5-Minute
Productivity
Workbook

5-Minute
Productivity
Workbook

Stop Procrastinating in just 5 Minutes a Day

SUSAN REYNOLDS

chartwell
books

This book belongs to:

....

Introduction

> "How long can you afford to put off who you really want to be?. . . From this instant on, vow to stop disappointing yourself. Separate yourself from the mob. Decide to be extraordinary and do what you need to do—now."
>
> Epictetus, *The Art of Living*

Are you among the many people currently suffering from a lack of productivity? If so, you're not alone. In a Franklin-Covey survey of more than 350,000 people, at all organizational levels, from around the world, respondents reported that they feel as if they are typically wasting 40 percent of their time.

With the advent of the Internet, email, instant messages, Zoom, social media, streaming services, and bringing our cell phones *everywhere*, it's also true that our ability to pay attention is under unprecedented attack. If you want to achieve anything beyond minimal efforts—whether at work or at home—it's more important than ever to learn how to focus your brain on the task at hand, as well as how to dive deeply into plotting your future.

Maybe you're one of those who are now working-at-home (determining your own schedule and how you use your time) or you're moving into our increasingly entrepreneurial culture (where you determine your own trajectory), or you're taking care of your family (and feeling super-stressed from busy schedules and endless demands). Whatever the current stressors of your life are, it will be imperative for you to master self-productivity. Even if you still have an office you go to daily, the days of simply fulfilling assigned tasks or a having a supervisor monitor your productivity are waning. Today, it's up to *you* to manage your time

and figure out what you want to accomplish and how you can best work towards achieving your short- and long-term goals. In short, what you accomplish within limited timeframes is up to you. It's also true that productivity is being given even more importance in corporate environments, with more companies using software programs to monitor their employees. Everyone expects employees to accomplish more, in a shorter amount of time. Those who dawdle may well be left behind.

And even if that isn't your precise situation, there is a common thread: all of us want to maximize the use of our time, to be both productive and accomplished, to fulfill our own expectations, to become the best version of ourselves, to meet all our responsibilities, or to achieve a lifelong dream. We all live in a fast-paced, highly connected world where anything is possible—if only you can find the time.

This handbook, therefore, is for anyone who wants to stop procrastinating and become more proficient and successful. It will help if you lost momentum during the COVID-19 pandemic, or if you have noticed waning productivity and simply want to perform better. It's also for anyone who seeks to expand their thinking when it comes to figuring out what they need to do to move forward in their ambitions.

Organized into 6 chapters, this book is designed to help you deeply probe your psyche, your thoughts, your emotions, and your ambitions to overcome procrastination and boost your personal productivity. Each introduces the most important concepts, and then offers a series of questions created to help you assess your situation. We'll begin with Where You Are Now (chapter 1) and Where You Want to Be (chapter 2), figuring out if your flagging productivity is a result of specific, recurring problems or of not being on the path you originally envisioned. Then, using elements from psychology, mindfulness, neuroscience, and other techniques for improving productivity, we'll focus on how you can Kick Your Nonproductive Habits (chapter 3), Maximize Your Brain's Thinking Capacity (chapter 4), and Improve Your Brain's Ability to Pay Attention (chapter 5). Towards the end, we'll discuss specific Practical Solutions (chapter 6) for becoming more productive, in your work responsibilities or in your personal life.

These pages will help you take a focused look at what's hampering your ability to be your best self, stop avoiding the tasks that need your attention, and aid you in designing an action plan for going forward. If this sounds daunting, before you panic, keep in mind that all the exercises in this handbook are designed to take only five minutes (per day) of your time. Set a timer, if you'd like, and work at your own pace, doing only what you can accomplish in those five minutes. Let's begin.

26%: the number of employees working remotely as of 2022	**6%:** the number of employees working remotely in 2018
92%: the number of employees who work remotely at least one day per week	**16%:** the number of companies that are fully remote
23%: the increase in the number of women working remotely since 2020	**15%:** the number of remote work opportunities
68%: the number of workers who would prefer to be fully remote	**45%:** the number of remote workers who would prefer a hybrid work arrangement
49%: the number of remote workers who would prefer to remain remote	**40%:** the number of workers who feel they've been more productive since working from home

CHAPTER 1

Where You Are Now

> "Some changes look negative on the surface, but you will soon realize that space is being created in your life for something new to emerge."
> Eckhart Tolle, *author*

For every change you desire to make—whether it's to rearrange your daily agenda so you get more accomplished, prioritize your life so you can achieve personal goals, change from slovenly and disorganized to organized and efficient, or sketch out a three-year plan for forging a new career—you'll be likelier to succeed if you figure out what specific, recurring problems are holding you back, or whether your flagging productivity has been trying to let you know that you're not where you want to be—jobwise, careerwise, or otherwise. If you ferret out the *real* reasons you might not be happy in your current situation, whether at work or at home, you won't waste months—or years—trying to be more efficient at something you don't really want to do.

First, let's examine your current situation and what you want to change about it. Then we'll consider why you haven't been able to enact change, before acknowledging those mistakes and moving on.

Is Fear of Change
Holding You Back?

Human brains were hardwired to focus on safety. From our earliest days, when daily life included the possibility of being eaten alive, our nervous systems (instinctive brains) focused on alerting and instinctively reacting to danger, while our prefrontal cortexes (thinking brains) focused on finding safe quarters, food to eat, water to drink, and people to keep us company.

Unfortunately, when it comes to making changes in your life, just the thought of shaking up what feels like a *safe* "status quo" feels threatening, which makes your hardwired (anxious) mind kick in, swiftly developing a list of reasons why you should stay right where you are, with what you know. Your thinking brain will add its chatter, likely focusing on potential risks, while discounting possible benefits. Thus, it requires *conscious thinking* to overcome fearful instincts and effect change. Before we leap in to figure out *why* you're struggling to make changes that will boost your productivity, let's explore your "status quo."

> If you do not change direction,
>
> *you may end up*
>
> *where you are going.*

Lao-Tzu, *Chinese philosopher*

ARE YOUR CURRENT RESPONSIBILITIES BRINGING YOU DOWN?

If you're struggling with productivity, you're likely not happy about something. This is an opportunity to be honest with yourself. Rather than responding immediately, take five minutes to think about each prompt that follows, considering what is happening in both your personal and your professional lives.

Jot down some things that come to mind about what you might be struggling with. (We'll narrow it down in a bit.)

_____

_____

_____

_____

_____

_____

_____

_____

_____

_____

_____

_____

_____

_____

_____

_____

_____

_____

WHAT SPECIFICALLY BUGS YOU?

Now let's peg what is getting under your skin. What is irritating you to the point that it's affected your productivity? Again, give this some thought and spend five minutes writing down the real reasons—not the superficial ones that first pop into your mind.

What's bugging you personally?

_____

_____

_____

_____

_____

_____

_____

_____

What's bugging you professionally?

_____

_____

_____

_____

_____

_____

_____

_____

ARE YOU FEELING FED UP?

If you're not being productive, it could be that you're experiencing one or more of the following:

→ You're frequently bored.
→ You'd rather procrastinate than do what's needed.
→ You're not feeling excited about anything you do.
→ You don't feel appreciated.
→ You're not using your natural abilities.
→ You don't see space to grow.
→ You no longer believe that what you're doing matters.

Feeling *fed up* signals that it's time to reassess how you're spending your time. The fault may not lie within you, but rather in what you've chosen—or *feel compelled*—to do with your time and energy.

If you're feeling "fed up," write about it here. Pinpoint what has really gotten under your skin lately.

_____

_____

_____

_____

_____

_____

_____

_____

_____

_____

_____

_____

5-Minute Checklist

Jack Canfield, a popular success coach and author, developed a "Difficult or Troubling Situation" exercise designed to help his clients identify and solve a problem that may be affecting their job satisfaction and figure out what they want to happen. He asks his coaching clients the following seven questions:

1. What is a difficult or troubling situation you are dealing with?
2. How are you creating or allowing it to happen?
3. What are you pretending not to know?
4. What is the payoff for keeping it like it is?
5. What would you rather be experiencing?
6. What actions will you take to create that?
7. By when will you take that action?

Choose something that's bugging you and take five minutes to go through the list now. You might just shake something loose that immediately improves your productivity.

What Would You
Immediately Change?

> "There comes a time when you ought to start doing what you want... If you keep taking jobs that you don't like because you think it will look good on your resume, isn't that a little like saving up sex for your old age?"
> Warren Buffett, *investor*

Now that you've identified where you're at, the first step in making any change is to clarify exactly *what* needs to change. Does even a minor shift feel threatening? Is a major shift required, and you're worried you're not up for it? Begin by listing ten changes you'd like to make that could bolster your productivity. You may want to make two lists, one for your work life and one for your personal life. Or simply focus on the one that's making you feel painfully bogged down and nonproductive; or make a list that incorporates both.

What needs to change?

1. _____
2. _____
3. _____
4. _____
5. _____
6. _____
7. _____
8. _____
9. _____
10. _____

WHY HAVE YOU CHOSEN STATUS QUO?

Beyond your brain's tendency to focus on minimizing risks, a lot of weird psychology also comes in to play when it's faced with change. Here are seven primary reasons you may find it so hard to change.

1. **Lack of motivation.** You don't feel sufficiently self-motivated and need a reason powerful enough to overcome mental, physical, or logistical obstacles or challenges.
2. **Nonproductive habits.** Your nonproductive habits hold you back and don't spark the kind of conscious thinking and purposeful action that precede change.
3. **Fear of the unknown.** You may feel just *comfortable enough* to hang on, but remaining in a "status quo" frame of mind limits opportunities to gain experience and become your best self.
4. **Lack of support.** You don't have a support system in place to cheer you on. We'll reveal later how you can become your own inner coach and *believe* in yourself.

I have accepted fear as part of life
—specifically, the fear of change.
I have gone ahead despite the pounding in the heart that says:
turn back.

Erica Jong, *feminist author*

5. **Self-doubt.** Your inner critic has convinced you that you're not good enough. No one really knows what they're doing when they start. Some leap, do, and learn; others wait, and wait, and wait.

6. **Focusing on others.** You're doing what you or others think you "should" do or you worry too much about how others may judge you. It's time to go about what you *must* do to make yourself happy.

7. **You don't feel worthy.** You've allowed someone else to judge your worth. Just like "there's no crying in baseball," there's no waiting in life. You are worthy, just as you are.

Luckily, you've bought this handbook, designed specifically to help you do the kind of conscious thinking and planning that will propel you to change what isn't working and bolster habits and strategies that will work to your advantage.

Take five minutes and pinpoint the reasons you might be resisting change. Write about how your coping methods have manifested in your life and how they might be holding you back.

_____

_____

_____

_____

_____

_____

_____

_____

_____

_____

_____

_____

WHAT OR WHO IS STOPPING YOU?

What stands in the way of your making the changes you want to make? Hint: it could be you! Are these physical realities, psychological obstacles within, obstacles arising from limitations, or are other people's needs and expectations keeping you stuck? Are these obstacles real, or something you fearfully imagine?

Take five minutes to assess the ten obstacles that you think stand in your way. Then, take another five and assess each one's potency. Should you cross it off and rethink? Can you see a way around it?

1. _____

2. _____

3. _____

4. _____

5. _____

6. _____

7. _____

8. _____

9. _____

10. _____

Every desire for change hears that little voice whispering, "I don't think so," or "that's not for me," or "it's too risky." Resistance often comes from insecurity, past failures, natural inertia, self-doubt, anxiety, indecision, or overthinking. Take just five minutes to probe what's behind your resistance. Once you know what it is, you can address it head-on or find a way to work around it.

NOTHING

is as painful as

staying stuck somewhere

you don't belong.

N.R. Narayana Murthy,
CEO and businessperson

WHY DO YOU KEEP SAYING "NO" TO YOURSELF?

Self-sabotage wreaks havoc with any attempt to change. When you decide to remain status quo, it can be helpful to examine the reasons you produce for why. When you know what you want to do, what you need to do, and how to go about it, *what stops you?*

Spend five minutes giving this some thought, then list five major reasons you tend to reject your own ideas about going forward.

1.

2.

3.

4.

5.

"All self-sabotage, lack of belief in ourselves, low self-esteem, judgments, criticism, and demands for perfection are forms of self-abuse in which we destroy the very essence of our vitality."
Deborah Adele, *author*

ARE YOU BEGINNING TO SEE A PATH FORWARD?

If you've illuminated what's bugging you and what you want to change, you have taken the first steps toward forging a new path, or at least new ways of going forward.

Take five minutes to write a brief statement about the changes you will make and how you'll go about it.

_____

_____

_____

_____

_____

_____

_____

_____

_____

_____

_____

_____

TIP

Start with something small that you can easily change, so your brain will experience what it feels like to succeed, then increase its desire to help by rewarding yourself for each change. If it feels good, your brain will want to do it again. Bolster your own willingness to change by becoming more comfortable with the process. When you're ready, it will be easier to go BIG.

Give Yourself a Break

Now that you've identified areas where you are not happy, discovered the reasons why you've been procrastinating on making changes, and noted what you want to change, it's important to forgive yourself for stalling. Yes, we all avoid and procrastinate, but it's nonproductive behavior and leads to negative self-talk. It's time to right the ship, so let's clear the decks by practicing self-compassion.

Compassion is different from feeling love or kindness—towards yourself or others. Self-compassion allows you to recognize the pain you have caused yourself and then offer yourself acceptance and forgiveness. When we offer ourselves compassion, we release the past and restore our dignity, while gifting us the flexibility to do better.

Every day the clock resets.

Your wins don't matter.

Your failures don't matter.

Don't stress on what was,

fight for what could be.

Sean Higgins,
professional basketball coach

5-MINUTE FORGIVENESS PLAN

Think about what you consider your worst nonproductivity "sin" and spend five minutes trying the following four essential steps to making a *sincere* apology:

1. Admit what you did wrong.
2. Explain why you regret your actions.
3. Acknowledge how it has hurt you.
4. Describe what you'll do in the future to avoid repeating your actions.

Write about each of the steps to make a sincere apology to yourself for your worst productivity "sin."

1. _____

_____

2. _____

_____

3. _____

_____

4. _____

_____

Now, read your written words and truly forgive yourself. Then congratulate yourself on taking an honest look at your challenges.

5-MINUTE SELF-COMPASSION MEDITATION

Sit quietly, slowly breathing in and out. Focus *only* on your breath, releasing all thoughts that try to interrupt. Keep doing this until you feel relaxed. Now, have your mind bring forth thoughts of forgiveness:

> "I forgive myself for needing as much time as I've needed."

> "I forgive myself for not clearly seeing what I needed to change."

> "I forgive myself for allowing fear to stop me."

> "I forgive myself for not trusting myself."

Then, breathe and release all negative, self-judgmental thoughts. Let them float away like butterflies disappearing into the sky.

Now, switch to positive statements:

> "My thoughts are clear and focused."

> "My ideas are wisely pointing me in the direction I want to go."

> "I will trust myself more."

> "I embrace change."

These are just examples—use whatever works best for you. Keep repeating the positive, self-affirming statements until you feel relaxed, then breathe slowly, cross your hands over your heart, and truly take them in.

The point is to release all negative thoughts about how long it's taken you to change. Forgiveness is the first step towards making the changes you desire.

Now that you've explored what's been holding you back from where you want to be, let's discuss the steps needed to boost your productivity—and help you get there.

Forgive yourself quickly
and as often as necessary.

Encourage yourself.

Tell yourself good things about yourself.

Melody Beattie, *author*

CHAPTER 2

Where You Want to Be

> "There is something in every one of you that waits and listens for the sound of the genuine in yourself."
> Howard Thurman, *philosopher*

If you're not productive, it may be that you're not *where* you want to be or *doing* what you most want to be doing. Could you be in the wrong marriage? Wrong community? Wrong job? Wrong profession? This section will help you stop frittering away time, seriously ponder your future, and focus on creating the life you want. Ultimately, you'll discover, *Where do you want to be?*

Have You Found *your Passion?*

You've heard it a million times: *If you love what you do, it doesn't feel like work.* That said, have *you* discovered your passion? If you haven't discovered what you most love to do, write down what brings you the most joy and consider if it's a passion that could influence what you do from here on. If you have more than one, write them all down on the following page.

Don't ask what the world needs.

Ask yourself what makes you come alive and then do that.

Because what the world needs is people who have *come alive.*

Howard Thurman, *philosopher*

What Would Life Look Like
if You Felt Successful?

Is your vision of success money-based? Service-based? Passion-based? What will your personal and/or professional lives look like when you *feel* enormously successful?

Ponder these questions, then spend five minutes writing down your unique vision of personal and professional success. Be as specific as possible.

_____

_____

_____

_____

_____

_____

_____

_____

_____

_____

_____

_____

_____

_____

_____

_____

_____

_____

_____

_____

WHAT WOULD THE PINNACLE OF SUCCESS LOOK LIKE?

Often, we simply don't dream far enough into our future. Beyond your definition of what success would look like for you now, take five minutes to ponder and write down a clear vision of what your life would look like if you achieved your ultimate vision of success.

_____

_____

_____

_____

_____

_____

_____

_____

_____

_____

_____

_____

_____

_____

_____

_____

_____

_____

_____

_____

_____

> "Never mind searching for who you are. Search for the person you aspire to be."
> Robert Breault, *opera singer*

Start Off by Picking a
Role Model

> "Success leaves clues."
> Anthony Robbins, *motivational speaker and author*

Role models help us visualize the differences between who we are now and who we'd like to become. Whether you want to be the CEO of a major company or the best tennis player in your local club, you can find a role model whose life choices can serve as a guidebook, their behavior as an ideal. A role model should be someone who excels, while also being respectful, hardworking, creative, free-thinking, altruistic, and moral; someone worth emulating, with the ideal qualities you'd like to develop.

Choose your role models carefully. Don't just pick famous people. Research your desired field or area of interest and find people who are doing what you'd love to do and doing it successfully, with intelligence, morals, and grace. Study how they got there and how they keep performing at peak capacity. Modeling your efforts to move in their *specific* direction can be extremely helpful.

List five people (alive or dead) whom you consider successful and think of as role models.

1. _____

2. _____

3. _____

4. _____

5. _____

Write down 1 to 3 reasons you consider each person successful.

Person 1

_____

_____

_____

Person 2

_____

_____

_____

Person 3

_____

_____

_____

Person 4

_____

_____

_____

Person 5

_____

_____

_____

Circle any words you used in stating those reasons that jump out to you. Are these the things you want for your life moving forward?

What can you learn from your role models about success?

_____

_____

_____

_____

_____

_____

_____

_____

_____

_____

_____

What qualities do they have that you need to develop? Be specific.

_____

_____

_____

_____

_____

_____

_____

_____

_____

_____

_____

_____

Next, Consider Your *Core Values*

You'll be most productive when you are doing something that feels meaningful to you. Make a list of core values that hold the most meaning for you. Core values might be protecting the planet, making a valuable contribution to society, helping others, sharing what you know or volunteering, teaching, obtaining financial security for your family, developing products (or raising children) that benefit the world.

Here's a list of possible core values, expressed in one word. When you write your core values on the next page, extend the description to illustrate how your core values would manifest.

Authenticity	Achievement	Adventure	Authority
Autonomy	Balance	Compassion	Challenge
Community	Competency	Contribution	Creativity
Curiosity	Faith	Growth	Honesty
Influence	Justice	Leadership	Learning
Meaningful Work	Openness	Optimism	Recognition
Respect	Security	Self-Respect	Service
Spirituality	Trustworthiness	Wealth	Wisdom

What are your top five core values?

1. _____

2. _____

3. _____

4. _____

5. _____

Why Core Values Matter

When you have a job, profession, or outside interest that matches your core values, it helps you:

- More fully express your authentic self.
- Continually grow as whole person.
- Feel more fully committed to what you're doing.
- Perform better individually and on teams.
- Feel more satisfied, engaged, and happy to stay.
- Increase your self-awareness.

Basically, when your core values are an integral part of what you do for a living (or to sustain your family), you become happier and more productive.

"I had chosen to use my work as a reflection of my values."
Sidney Poitier, *actor*

ARE YOU ALIGNED OR *MISALIGNED*?

If your current responsibilities are not aligned with your core values, this could be a major reason for procrastination, lack of fulfillment, a feeling of drudgery, or an absence of joy. Take the following five-minute assessments to see where you stand.

5-MINUTE ALIGNMENT ASSESSMENT

Are your current responsibilities aligned with your core values? If so, how?

_____

_____

_____

_____

_____

Write down what makes your current responsibilities misaligned with your core values and passion.

_____

_____

_____

_____

_____

_____

_____

5-MINUTE ALIGNMENT ASSESSMENT

Can you integrate your core values into what you are doing now? If so, write down 3 to 5 ways you can align your values with your current responsibilities.

_____

_____

_____

_____

_____

_____

_____

_____

_____

_____

_____

_____

_____

_____

_____

_____

_____

_____

_____

_____

_____

LOOK FOR WAYS TO INTEGRATE YOUR CORE VALUES

What would you *love* to contribute to the world? Besides making money (which we all must do), what could you *ideally choose* to do that would benefit your family, your community, or the larger world?

Take five minutes to identify at least ten professions, jobs, or activities that would bolster your core values. If your concern is your personal life, include things you could do that would bolster your core values, such as volunteering. Note that these could also be ten activities you wish to teach your children.

1. _____

2. _____

3. _____

4. _____

5. _____

6. _____

7. _____

8. _____

9. _____

10. _____

> "Life is good when you live from your roots. Your values are a critical source of energy, enthusiasm, and direction. Work is meaningful and fun when it's an expression of your true core."
> Shoshana Zuboff, *social psychologist*

Now Consider Your
Primary Wants

To really figure out what they genuinely want (core values) and whether they *genuinely* want it (motivation impetus), leadership coach Rich Litvin suggests that his clients make a list of "100 wants." So, let's try it. It can be anything you want, whether it's possessions, career aspirations, money, love, a safe neighborhood, a flush local food bank, a flower garden filled with lilies, a month in Tuscany, world peace, or something similar. The first task may take five sessions of five minutes each, but then you should be able to break each succeeding task down to five minutes. Here's how it works:

STEP 1. On the following pages, produce a list of 100 things you want—from a new car to world peace. This will take some time, but it's worth it, particularly when you need to think harder to finally reach 100. With each listing, be as specific as possible.

STEP 2. Add category labels to each item. You decide what labels and how many. They could be THINGS, CAREER, HOME, HEALTH, LOVE, CONNECTION, COMMUNITY, WORLD. This will help you identify the wants that may be more realistic, immediate, and achievable, versus the ones that are aspirational, only achievable over a long period of time, or with help.

STEP 3. Now, pare down your list to only those things that you consider a definite want. A definite, something you truly desire. Basically, you are rating your wants to identify what's profoundly important to you.

STEP 4. Reflect on what your list shows you, by answering the questions that follow, starting on page 52. This is all designed to help you narrow down your values and your most potent wants for yourself. Together with your talents, this will help you identify what will make you both happier and more productive.

Want

CATEGORY

1.

2.

3.

4.

5.

6.

7.

8.

9.

10.

Want

CATEGORY

11.

12.

13.

14.

15.

16.

17.

18.

19.

20.

Want

CATEGORY

21.

22.

23.

24.

25.

26.

27.

28.

29.

30.

Want

CATEGORY

31.

32.

33.

34.

35.

36.

37.

38.

39.

40.

Want

CATEGORY

41.

42.

43.

44.

45.

46.

47.

48.

49.

50.

Want

CATEGORY

51.

52.

53.

54.

55.

56.

57.

58.

59.

60.

Want

CATEGORY

61.

62.

63.

64.

65.

66.

67.

68.

69.

70.

Want

CATEGORY

71.

72.

73.

74.

75.

76.

77.

78.

79.

80.

Want

CATEGORY

81.

82.

83.

84.

85.

86.

87.

88.

89.

90.

Want

CATEGORY

91.

92.

93.

94.

95.

96.

97.

98.

99.

100.

What does your pared-down list show about you?

_____

_____

_____

_____

_____

Does it strongly reflect your core values? Which ones? Be specific.

1. _____

2. _____

3. _____

4. _____

5. _____

6. _____

Do you see a pattern? Are you more focused on career, or values? Is money your primary motivator? Do you have altruistic obsessions? Are your wants focused on your personal life, revealing areas that clearly need attention?

_____

_____

_____

_____

_____

_____

CREATE A LIST OF WANTS TO ACHIEVE

Keeping the work you've done to learn more about what you want in mind, take five minutes to ponder specific wants you will manifest. Remember to think immediate and achievable, or at least achievable within five years.

Identify your specific, achievable wants.

1. _____
2. _____
3. _____
4. _____
5. _____
6. _____
7. _____
8. _____
9. _____
10. _____

You will recognize your own path when you come upon it, *because you will suddenly have all the energy and imagination you will ever need.*

Jerry Gillies, *The MoneyLove Manifesto*

Which specific, achievable goals do you want to focus on immediately?

1.

2.

3.

4.

5.

What steps would you need to take?

1.

2.

3.

4.

5.

It's Time to Think About *Options*

This is where you start to envision what you could choose to do. Now that you've thought about your level of happiness and the passion that might make your responsibilities feel much lighter and far easier to achieve, it's time to focus on what you could do.

Spend five minutes listing ten things you could choose to do—personally or professionally—that would make you feel more energetic, more focused, more motivated, happier, and eventually more successful, according to your specific goals and values. This is a preliminary list of options, so go a little crazy and think BIG, wild, ridiculous.

1. _____

2. _____

3. _____

4. _____

5. _____

6. _____

7. _____

8. _____

9. _____

10. _____

PAUSE FOR A REALITY CHECK

Do *not* toss out the wild and crazy ideas you just listed—but do pause to further consider what's achievable. Pick the top five ideas that may seem out of reach and think expansively. If not an acrobat, how about a physical therapist or a massage therapist? A gymnastics teacher? A playground supervisor?

Top five ideas:

1. _____

2. _____

3. _____

4. _____

5. _____

Write five alternatives for your top five options.

1. _____

   _____

2. _____

   _____

3. _____

   _____

4. _____

   _____

5. _____

   _____

If you limit choices to only what seems possible or reasonable, *you disconnect yourself from what you truly want,* and all that is left is a *compromise.*

Robert Fritz, *The Path of Least Resistance*

Turn Your Dreams into Reality

Knowing what you want and how soon you want it to happen helps you focus and harness not only your time and energy, but your brain's most potent thinking processes. To get all parts of you on board, take five minutes to identify and list new life goals that are positive, specific, and achievable.

What are now your long-term, life goals?

1. _____
2. _____
3. _____
4. _____
5. _____
6. _____
7. _____
8. _____
9. _____
10. _____

> "A dream written down with a date becomes a goal. A goal broken down into steps becomes a plan. A plan backed by action makes your dreams come true."
> Dr. Greg S. Reid, *Think and Grow Rich*

CREATE A MISSION STATEMENT

Corporations use mission statements to determine precisely who they are, what they want to achieve, and how they will get there, while staying true to their core values. They use their mission statement to support their employees (you), motivate their employees (also you), establish values, plan strategically, and understand why their business exists. Now that you have your life goals identified, write your own mission statement to clearly state:

1. Who you are. What you love to do.
2. What you value most. What will bring you the most satisfaction.
3. What *specifically* you most want to accomplish (both right now and long-term).

Use this space to keep revising and editing until you have a focused, clear statement. Then write it on an index card and tape it to your bathroom mirror. Use it as a daily affirmation until it's ingrained in your psyche.

_____

_____

_____

_____

_____

_____

_____

_____

_____

_____

_____

_____

_____

_____

_____

_____

CREATE A VISION STATEMENT

Now that you've established your core values, identified your life goals, and created a potent mission statement, you need a vision statement that outlines the steps needed to advance toward your goals. A vision statement focuses on long-term goals. Remember, you can always adjust this (you should always be adjusting this!), so start with what you know now (or do research, if you like). A vision statement might go as follows:

→ In the next three years, I want to transition into nonprofit management, which will be a new career.

→ Once I delineate what I need to learn to advance towards that profession, I will sign up for classes beginning next fall.

As you progress, update your vision statement.

"Our goals can only be reached through the vehicle of a plan, in which we must fervently believe, and upon which we must fervently act. There is no other route to success."
Pablo Picasso, *artist*

5-Minute Focus

Your brain's reticular cortex serves as the gatekeeper for stimuli, either helping you pay attention to what matters or making you easily distracted. Train it to identify what will help you obtain your goals by spending five minutes *every day* focusing specifically on what you most want to happen. (Working on your vision plan, researching, and studying will all help with this.) This trains your brain to weed out what doesn't matter, while focusing more on what does.

CREATE AN ACTION PLAN

To achieve goals, you need an "action plan." Choose your highest priority goal and spend five minutes breaking down the steps you'll need to advance towards it. Then, you can proceed to do the same for your other goals. You can't barrel forward on everything so prioritize.

Write your step-by-step action plan to achieve your most important goal here:

1. _____

2. _____

3. _____

4. _____

5. _____

6. _____

7. _____

8. _____

Now, go back and order the tasks. Start with the easiest ones to accomplish, if possible. That way you get to experience a sense of accomplishment along the way. Also, give yourself a timeline for getting each task done, and use these pages to monitor your progress.

1. _____

Timeline: _____

2. _____

Timeline: _____

3. _____

Timeline: _____

4. _____

Timeline: _____

5. _____

Timeline: _____

6. _____

Timeline: _____

7. _____

Timeline: _____

8. _____

Timeline: _____

"Have a bias towards action—let's see something happen now. You can break that big plan into small steps and take the first step right away."
Indira Gandhi, *politician*

Are You Using *Your Superpower?*

According to Gallup, two of the most important predictors of employee retention and satisfaction are using your *top strengths* at work and your manager recognizing those top strengths. And yet, a study in the *Journal of Positive Psychology* showed that only about one-third of people can identify their own strengths. Even more disheartening, only 17 percent of people use their strengths most of the time each day. (This also applies if you are currently managing a home or raising children, as you may not be recognizing your own valuable skills and contributions.) So, *what's your superpower, and are you maximizing it?* Let's find out.

List some skills you already have.

1. _____

2. _____

3. _____

4. _____

5. _____

6. _____

7. _____

8. _____

9. _____

10. _____

> "An excellent person is never excellent enough.
> True excellence comes from continued striving."
> Mike Hayes, *former SEAL*

This one makes a net;

this one stands and wishes.

Would you like to make a bet

which one gets the fishes.

Chinese proverb

List the top five skills required for your desired job, career, or activity.

1. _____
2. _____
3. _____
4. _____
5. _____

List the top five skills you need to develop to go where you want to go.

1. _____
2. _____
3. _____
4. _____
5. _____

Maximize Brain Capacity

Your brain continues to grow and change throughout your life. It can repair damaged regions, reassign tasks to a healthier area, grow new neurons, discard neurons not in use, rewire existing connections, and create complex new networks to master new skills. What you *choose* to do—think, read, study, practice—affects how your brain either grows or shrinks, expands or contracts, learns or stagnates. Stimulate your brain to maximize your genius.

List five ways you can improve your skills.

1. _____

2. _____

3. _____

4. _____

5. _____

Identify five places where you can acquire skills.

1. _____

2. _____

3. _____

4. _____

5. _____

Sign up for whatever classes you might need (or hire a tutor), watch online tutorials, ask for help, and practice your new skills until they become second nature. Soon, you'll be ready to make that massive leap forward.

5-Minute Superpower Quiz

According to Robert Biswas-Diener, executive coach and managing director of Positive Acorn, you may be blind to what your personal strengths are because what others see as extraordinary you live with daily, and therefore think of as ordinary. To make sure you're not discounting your secret superpower, ask contemporaries to write down what they see as your strengths and have them slip the pieces of paper into an envelope that you'll open later.

Now that you've pondered your passion, your dreams, and your wants to obtain a clearer vision of where you want to be, let's move on to discuss methods for breaking any nonproductive habits that may be holding you back.

Courage is your natural setting.

You do not need to become courageous, but rather peel back the layers of self-protective, limiting beliefs that keep you small.

Vironika Tugaleva, *The Love Mindset*

CHAPTER 3

Kick Your Nonproductive Habits

"We are so scared of being judged that we look for every excuse to procrastinate."
Erica Jong, *Seducing the Demon: Writing for My Life*

The American Psychological Association defines self-regulation as the ability to control your behavior and manage your thoughts and emotions in appropriate ways. While self-control is all about controlling and inhibiting impulses, self-regulation refers to the many ways people *choose* how they act to achieve desired goals and to function in socially acceptable ways. Examples would include:

→ Managing intense emotions like frustration, disappointment, embarrassment, or anger.

→ Calming down after something exciting or upsetting has happened.

→ Refocusing attention after finishing one task and starting another, or when disturbed.

→ Managing potentially harmful impulses.

→ Behaving appropriately and getting along well with other people.

When it comes to productivity concerns, one of the primary problems most of us face is procrastination, which is often a failure to self-regulate our anxiety.

Get a Grip on Procrastination

> "Begin doing what you want to do now. We are not living in eternity. We have only this moment, sparkling like a star in our hand—and melting like a snowflake."
> Francis Bacon, *philosopher and the Father of Pragmatism*

According to Timothy Pychyl, Ph.D., a Canadian researcher and author of two books on procrastination, a tendency to procrastinate is not necessarily the result of poor time-management skills. It's important to reiterate that: *Procrastination isn't necessarily the result of poor time management.* Pychyl says procrastination is often a failure to regulate our emotions (particularly anxiety) and acts as "a gap between *intention* and *action*, when you know what you have to do, but cannot bring yourself to do it." Reasons he suggests people might procrastinate:

1. You'll do anything to avoid stress. Eventually, you become "task-averse," which could lead to chronic procrastination. We'll reveal ways to modulate stress levels later.

2. You're so afraid of failure your "fight or flight" hormones kick in, and you opt for "flight" (avoidance). You need to bolster self-esteem, which we're working on here.

3. You don't know how to do it well and succumb to inertia. You don't want to admit to your shortcomings. Studies show most people would rather others think them lazy than incompetent. Up your skills!

4. You focus on the negative aspects. When you hate to do it, you put it off. If you purposefully identify the positive aspects of getting it done, you can regulate your motivation.

5. You set expectations too high, or you set goals too high, making it impossible to achieve them, which leads to self-criticism, which leads to more avoidance. Think *progress* not perfection.

6. You suffer from low self-esteem. The fear of how your performance will be judged cripples your ability to act. Keep working your way through this handbook and you'll see progress.

7. You suffer from learned helplessness. You didn't learn self-regulation as a child and feel helpless facing complicated tasks. But you *can* learn resourcefulness (what this handbook is about).

8. You learned to rebel through inaction. Your overbearing parent(s) didn't foster self-efficacy so you lack confidence in your abilities, but you're an adult now, so it's time to accept responsibility.

9. You imagine a future self will be more capable. You're using mind trickery, waiting for a magical outcome—unless you're *actively* working on your skillset. We're helping you become who you want to be now.

10. You lack "executive" functions. You haven't trained your brain to be decisive, organized, task-oriented, focused, and efficient, all skills you can develop and thereby *self-regulate*. Some self-regulation deficiencies include:

    → You don't break it down. If it's too complex, you allow your feelings of overwhelm to help you avoid the task.

    → You don't establish or respond to deadlines. Often deadlines are easier to meet if a boss assigns them, but you can learn the discipline to set and meet your own.

    → You allow yourself to be distracted. Between 1978 and now, procrastination has jumped 15 percent in workplaces, due to distractions like the Internet and personal cell phones.

    → You don't identify a motivating reason. Find a reason to light a fire under you.

TIP

Don't rely on stress hormones. Some people justify their procrastination by saying they love the energy last-minute pressure brings. Unfortunately, if they consistently wait until the task requires a massive surge of energy, they are conjuring a dependence on adrenaline and cortisone, stress-related hormones that could become problematic.

Important Note

There are reasons for procrastination that may reflect psychological or neurological issues, such as clinical depression, debilitating anxiety, or attention deficit hyperactivity disorder (ADHD). Some people may not fall into pathological categories but may still suffer from firmly entrenched neurological patterns that reinforce procrastination to the point that they need outside help to break the habit. If you might fall into those categories, it may be beneficial to seek professional help.

Think Highly of Yourself

Chronic procrastinators often report lower self-esteem, greater public self-consciousness, and social anxiety. They also report a more diffused sense of self than achievers and a stronger tendency toward self-sabotage. Though they are equal in verbal and abstract thinking abilities to achievers, they are often anxious, avoidant, and fearful of being evaluated based on ability.

My mother always told me I wouldn't amount to anything because I procrastinate.

I said, *Just wait.*

Judy Tenuta, *comedian*

Figure Out Why *You* Procrastinate

During the recent global pandemic, we experienced massive stress, which led many people to feel a lack of motivation to do much of anything. We all procrastinated, which seemed like a reasonable self-care decision. Even in normal circumstances, everyone puts off doing something, but if you still regularly procrastinate on essential tasks, it's time to examine why.

5-MINUTE PROCRASTINATION BUSTER

Ponder some situations in which you most often procrastinate. No self-bashing, which can increase procrastination, only notice *why* you stall. Once you know why, you can begin to address the underlying problem and formulate ways to break the habit. When you settle on five situations, take five minutes to answer the prompts, either five minutes for each prompt, or five minutes altogether—it's up to you.

List five situations where you're most likely to procrastinate.

1.

2.

3.

4.

5.

What excuses do you typically make? What are your "go-to" reasons for procrastinating or putting things off? Is there any truth to what you tell yourself?

1. _____

2. _____

3. _____

4. _____

5. _____

When it's something you just don't want to do, what do you choose to do instead? Identifying these actions may help you realize when you're procrastinating.

1. _____

2. _____

3. _____

4. _____

5. _____

5-Minute Brain Focus

Your brain can serve as a spotlight (seeing a large perimeter) or a flashlight (focusing a beam of light on a subject). When you need to focus and simply can't, imagine your brain as a flashlight focusing a beam of bright light on whatever it is that has you stymied. You may find that the "extra light" on the subject instantly improves your focus.

How do you feel when you procrastinate? We're not talking about surface feelings. How do you feel about your inability to expeditiously complete work that matters to you?

_____

_____

_____

_____

Do you berate or punish yourself? How?

_____

_____

_____

_____

_____

What are your worst thoughts about yourself when it happens?

Are these thoughts a fair assessment? Why or why not?

Do you procrastinate often? Are you worried about it?

Four Signs of Procrastination Overkill

Four signs your procrastination has become a problem you may not be able to solve alone are:

1. It's chronic, extensive, and feels compulsive.
2. You're constantly putting your home or job at risk.
3. You lie to cover up the fact you haven't even begun the work.
4. You procrastinate in all areas of your life, including with friends.

If these are true of you, *please seek help*. You can learn to overcome your debilitating habits, but it may be hard to do so on your own.

15-20%: the number of adults affected by chronic procrastination

25%: the number of adults who feel procrastination is their defining personality trait

57%: the number of unemployed people who self-identify as procrastinators

Stop Letting Limiting Beliefs
Slow You Down

Limiting beliefs are those thoughts we harbor that hold us back. They can be universal "truths" we believe (even when we don't know of a reliable source), or personal beliefs we formulated long before we were mature enough to assess whether they were true. Limiting beliefs decrease self-esteem. The ten most common limiting beliefs are:

1. I'm too old.
2. I'm not smart enough.
3. I am not educated enough.
4. I'm afraid of trying and failing.
5. You must have money to make money.
6. I've already tried everything.
7. I can't do that.
8. I don't feel I really deserve it.
9. I'll never be able to do that.
10. *All* the good ones are taken.

These, of course, are too generic, and easily countered. The ones you tend to harbor about how you handle your responsibilities will be far more specific and not so easily countered.

Spend five minutes thinking about and then listing specific "limiting beliefs" you harbor about yourself. These would be beliefs about your competency or ability to do what is required of you.

1. _____

2. _____

3. _____

4. _____

5. _____

 5-Minute Belief Assessment

Limiting beliefs about your abilities often have repetitious, identifiable effects. Take five minutes to write about how your limiting beliefs affect your ability to perform. Can you see how long-held, low assessments have limited your performance? Try not to judge your previous beliefs; instead, upgrade them to what you now know about your abilities.

KICK THOSE OLD BELIEFS TO THE CURB

Once you've identified your limiting beliefs, the best way to counter them is to refute them by stating something positive that you do know. If one of your beliefs is that you are inadequate to the task, perhaps you can simply state that you *can learn* to handle the task efficiently.

Write five statements that contradict your limiting beliefs.

1. _____

2. _____

3. _____

4. _____

5. _____

 5-Minute Affirmation Session

Spend five minutes changing your contradiction statements into affirmations (simple, positive statements that accurately assess your abilities). Write them down on an index card and then read each one several times. Keep the card near your bed and read them every morning for a month.

NOTCH UP YOUR SELF-ESTEEM

We're going to discuss more concrete strategies for combatting procrastination later (after we address other reasons your productivity is not up to par), but for now let's counteract the negativity you've just probed by doing a few exercises to boost your self-esteem.

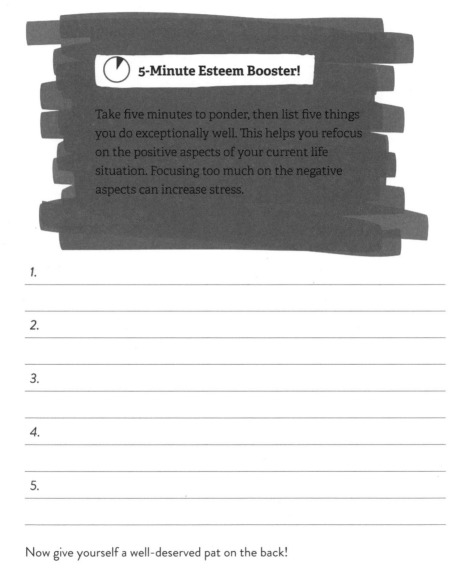

5-Minute Esteem Booster!

Take five minutes to ponder, then list five things you do exceptionally well. This helps you refocus on the positive aspects of your current life situation. Focusing too much on the negative aspects can increase stress.

1. _____

2. _____

3. _____

4. _____

5. _____

Now give yourself a well-deserved pat on the back!

Give yourself credit: Take a full five minutes to think about and then list five ways you make a valuable contribution at work (or home). Go ahead, give yourself a little credit, or better yet, another hearty pat on the back.

1. _____

2. _____

3. _____

4. _____

5. _____

Why You Want Self-Efficacy

Mastery of skills creates *self-efficacy*, the belief that you can meet your goals by the actions you take. Repeated mastery develops the kind of stamina, focus, and confidence that bolsters your ability to successfully perform tasks. With equal talents and smarts, those with less self-efficacy don't perform as well as those who have strong self-efficacy. Here's how it helps:

- **Less avoidance.** Facing challenges doesn't feel as daunting.
- **Better performance.** Less self-doubt and more confidence boosts your positivity: you *can* do this and do it well.
- **Greater self-esteem.** Success breeds success.
- **Less anxiety, depression, stress.** Confidence saves the day!

If you lack self-efficacy, improve your skills. If you need outside help, ask for it. If you are constantly frustrated, address the causes. Find ways to meet a series of goals, increase your self-efficacy, and boost your productivity.

List five ways you could bolster your confidence. Are there things you could do that would immediately make you feel better about yourself?

1.
   _____

2.
   _____

3.
   _____

4.
   _____

5.
   _____

List five ways to provide self-care. Self-care helps calm frazzled nerves. Self-care might look like taking a nap, taking a weekend off, taking a hot bath, asking for help on a few tasks, or even hiring someone to help.

1.
   _____

2.
   _____

3.
   _____

4.
   _____

5.
   _____

Use Cognitive Behavioral Therapy
to Stop Nonproductive Thoughts

> "You have considerable power to construct self-helping thoughts, feelings, and actions... You have the ability, if you use it, to choose healthy instead of unhealthy thinking, feeling, and acting."
> Albert Ellis, *psychotherapist*

Cognitive Behavioral Therapy (CBT) theorizes that psychological distress results from distorted thinking about stimuli (which we'll discuss later in depth) and uses techniques designed to break the cycle of nonproductive thinking. *You can also use this technique to address anxiety,* those nagging, self-defeating thoughts that cripple efficacy. Four simple CBT tactics you can use when feeling stressed, fearful, anxious, insecure, or similar nonproductive emotions are:

1. Recognize conscious (and uproot unconscious) automatic thoughts that keep your mind stuck in a nonproductive rut.
2. Disperse a negative thought by clearly stating contradictory evidence.
3. Create an explanation that refutes the original negative thought.
4. If the first three strategies don't work, simply think about something else.

CBT is considered "the gold standard" in the psychotherapy field.

5-MINUTE THOUGHT BUSTERS

Now, let's put this knowledge to practical use. Take five minutes *on each question* to focus on and write the particulars, pinpointing any negative thoughts or beliefs underneath your emotions.

Begin by remembering a recent time when you felt upset or behaved in a way contradictory to your goals.

_____

_____

_____

_____

_____

_____

_____

_____

_____

_____

_____

_____

_____

_____

_____

_____

_____

Now, realistically assess your thoughts at the time. Were they realistic? What would have been closer to the truth?

_____

_____

_____

_____

_____

_____

_____

_____

_____

Why do you think you behaved the way you did? What is it about the situation or the people involved that caused your distress?

_____

_____

_____

_____

_____

_____

_____

_____

_____

_____

Can you identify which conscious or unconscious beliefs about yourself, others, or the situation may have caused you to react the way you did?

_____

_____

_____

_____

_____

_____

_____

_____

_____

_____

With the clearer vision a calmer mindset brings, how would you reframe those beliefs, or think about this type of situation differently?

_____

_____

_____

_____

_____

_____

_____

_____

_____

_____

Now, envision a far more positive script for this type of event. In a comparable situation, how would you now choose to behave to effect success for all concerned?

_____

_____

_____

_____

_____

_____

_____

_____

_____

_____

Stop in the Name of Sanity

Negative thoughts often pop into our brains, far faster and more often than positive thoughts. If you've tried all the CBT techniques and you're still struggling to tamp down negative thoughts, try just saying "STOP." If you're not alone, thinking "STOP" or simply holding up your hand to mimic "STOP" will work. Keep doing this and eventually you'll automatically stop errant negative thoughts from intruding.

Transform Your Inner Critic
into Your Inner Coach

> "I've been all over the world and
> I've never seen a statue of a critic."
> Leonard Bernstein, *conductor and composer*

We all have that nagging voice inside, the one that criticizes the way we look, think, and act. It's one of the biggest productivity thieves. It works against you every time—*as does anxiety*. Jack Canfield, author of *The Success Principles*, recommends turning that inner *critic* into your inner *coach*. He says most of our critics result from someone angrily addressing our faulty thinking, such as a parent scolding a child for running into a street without looking. Under the anger (the critic) are three messages (the coach) that Canfield says it's important to hear:

Fear	I'm afraid you'll get hit by a car and be badly hurt.
Requests	Please pay closer attention, be aware of danger, be more careful in the future.
Love	You are so precious to me that I would be lost without you. I want you to be safe and healthy.

To transform your inner critic into your inner coach, whenever you fail to accomplish a task you need or want to do, practice Canfield's Four Steps to Making Change:

1. Express how angry you are with yourself for what you perceive as negative behavior.
2. Identify the fear behind your anger: What are you afraid will happen if you don't improve?
3. Ask yourself to do better. Make a positive suggestion. Write it as an affirmation.
4. Express the love you feel for yourself, as motivation for change.

So, let's try one:

Think of something you did that disappointed you. Take five minutes to relive it in depth and write about the situation, keeping in mind the anger, fear, and requests embedded in your negative self-judgment.

_____

_____

_____

_____

_____

_____

_____

_____

_____

_____

_____

_____

Practice saying, "Thank you for your concern and feedback," to your inner coach, tell them that you're sorry you screwed up (you're learning!), then ask your coach what they *fear* will happen if you do this, or something similar, again. Spend five minutes listing those fears; they're instructive!

Ask your inner coach what specific actions *they would like to see you do to address this situation/flaw/problem/emotion? Spend your five minutes developing specifics.*

1. _____

2. _____

3. _____

4. _____

5. _____

Ask your inner coach how this change will benefit or serve *you now and in the future. Be specific.*

1. _____

2. _____

3. _____

4. _____

5. _____

Use this transformation process for recurring problem areas or instances in which faulty thinking thwarts your attempts to be productive; soon your coach will offer up creative solutions and positive ways of thinking that make it far easier for you to stay on course.

It's Not Just You

America Online and Salary.com surveyed 10,000 USA employees in 2019 and found that the average 8-hour-a-day worker "fritters away" 2.09 hours per day, *not* counting lunch hour. Nearly 45 percent of workers slack via personal Internet use (email, IM, online polls, interactive games, or chat rooms). Socializing ran second (23.4 percent of respondents), followed by conducting personal business, "spacing out," running errands, and making personal phone calls. Some employers factor a wasted hour into salary offers, but hope socializing or creative mind-wandering leads to innovation. All this to let you know that you're not alone in procrastinating, and that utilizing the techniques you're learning here will help you maximize use of your time at work (or on task).

TIP Check your mindset. When facing a challenge, do you put too much pressure on yourself? Do you approach each task expecting to fail? Do you feel overwhelmed before you even start? These negative mindsets can make it far harder to productively forge ahead. If you tend to think negatively, work on challenging your inner thoughts and replacing them with affirmations.

Turn Bad Habits into *Good Habits*

Habits are usually triggered behaviors that you've done so often that your brain's automatic, sensory-motor system kicks in, leading you to unconsciously repeat the behaviors. Habits become rote, something your brain has decided must be something you chose to streamline your life. Thus, entrenched habits don't even engage your prefrontal (thinking) cortex. It's worse during times of stress, as your prefrontal cortex essentially goes offline during those times.

When it comes to productive, beneficial habits, rote behavior works fine, but if you have a nonproductive, destructive habit that is harming you, failure to engage your thinking cortex works against your best efforts to break those bad habits.

To engage your prefrontal cortex, bring *full focus* to the choices you are making in the present moment. Make the habit you want to break mindful—and increasingly less automatic—gifting you time to *consciously choose* a more productive behavior.

Habits work so smoothly that we hardly ever think about them.

The world of (undesirable) habits is so self-contained, it's helpful to think of it as a kind of *'second self'*—

a part of you that lives in the shadow cast by the thinking mind you know so well.

Wendy Wood, *Good Habits, Bad Habits*

Persist!

Research suggests that behaviors often require varying amounts of repetition before becoming automatic: Altering your drink choices from unhealthy to healthy could take 59 days; adding a healthier food choice in place of junk food may take as long as 65 days; and the biggest nut of all, of course, is exercising, which may take more than 90 days. Get a calendar and mark the number of days suggested then keep going until you reach the end, and then it will likely be so ingrained, you won't stop doing it.

Also, use *mindfulness* (discussed in chapter 5) to bring your attention to exactly what you're doing. For example, as you reach for the bag of cheesy snacks, simply notice your behavior, then pause to ask yourself: *Why? Why am I desiring cheesy snacks? Why now? Am I angry? Sad? Frustrated? Bored?* Once you identify the triggers that lead you to the pantry, you can stop yourself from unconsciously behaving the same every time. Instead, you can *consciously choose* an alternative, healthier way to cope.

"A behavior happens when three elements of MAP—Motivation, Ability, and Prompt—come together at the same time. Motivation is your desire to do the behavior. Ability is your capacity to do the behavior. And Prompt is your cue to do the behavior."
B.J. Fogg, Ph.D., *Tiny Habits: The Small Changes that Change Everything*

5-Minute Reward Behaviors

Whenever you employ a conscious choice that benefits rather than harms you, pause to notice how good it felt for your body, mind, and soul. *Reward yourself* for the positive, helpful behavior by doing something you enjoy that's also beneficial to you, such as pausing to sit outside and watch the sunset, playing catch with your child or your dog, doing a sun salutation yoga pose, or brewing a cup of lavender tea. Keep reinforcing the more helpful behavior. If food is your issue, employ conscious choice in the grocery store, and soon you'll stop buying foods and drinks that thwart your attempts to make healthier choices. The same ideas hold true for habits that keep you from being productive.

5-MINUTE HABIT SPOTLIGHT

Take five minutes to contemplate bad habits you've developed that consistently thwart your productivity.

List nonproductive habits you want to break.

1. _____

2. _____

3. _____

4. _____

5. _____

Go the Extra Mile

An analytics company examined 7.5 million cell phones to find out how far people would travel to consistently work out at a gym. Those with an average round trip of 3.7 miles worked out five or more times a month, while those with an average round trip of 5.1 miles went only once. That's a noticeably short difference in distance for such a huge decrease in workout sessions. The next time you're creating a new habit, go the extra mile.

5-MINUTE MOTIVATION EXERCISE

Using the list you created on the previous page, spend five minutes on each question below. Delving into your reasons for change and devising methods to change will boost your motivation.

Identify why you want to change each bad habit listed on the previous page. Be specific about your reasons, as you need sufficient motivation to make lasting change.

1. _____

2. _____

3. _____

4. _____

5. _____

Now spend five minutes thinking about, then listing the method you'll use to change each nonproductive habit. Think strategically.

1. _____
2. _____
3. _____
4. _____
5. _____

Create a cue that helps you consciously choose productive habits. For example, some people use inspirational messages or quotes, some people create a "To Do" list for each day, some people use a "do not disturb" sign to indicate that focused productivity is in process.

1. _____

2. _____

3. _____

4. _____

5. _____

Remember to REWARD yourself for the good habits you choose. Reinforcing productive choices will make them easier to choose and eventually make them rote. Now that you've worked on kicking any nonproductive habits, it's time to discover ways to maximize your brain's working capacity.

TIP

If you need assistance to break a bad habit, fire up your frontal cortex or "thinking brain" to produce creative ways to cue yourself. For example, if perusing your phone late into the night is keeping you from falling asleep, try setting a timer for the ideal time to turn it off for the night.

CHAPTER 4

Maximize Your Brain's Thinking

> "The significant problems we face cannot be solved by the same level of thinking that created them."
> Albert Einstein, Nobel Prize–winning physicist

Your brain is a miraculous "computer," but it's up to you to maximize its capacity. You have to teach your frontal cortex how you want it to think. One way to begin is by identifying the faulty ways you've learned to think.

Disrupt Faulty Thinking

Unfortunately, many situations—especially new or challenging ones—can make us feel anxious, which then affects our ability to think clearly. In those first few anxious moments, we may succumb to envisioning the worst possible outcome, imagining that others don't want us to succeed, that we are not up to the task, that what we are being asked to do is punitive. This kind of fear-based, faulty thinking negatively impacts your productivity—but it's not the only faulty thinking that can slow you down. Here are ten forms of fear-based, nonproductive thinking that can trip you up:

1. **Catastrophizing:** You turn something potentially harmless into something catastrophic—often before it happens. You overestimate what *might* happen and underestimate your ability to do your best work under duress.

2. **Filtering:** Your boss compliments you on a project, then points out one small flaw. You focus on the flaw, assume they didn't like your work, *filtering in* the negativity and *filtering out* the praise.

3. **Black and White Thinking:** You judge everything in extremes: right or wrong; disastrous or perfect. There's no middle ground for your, or anyone else's, thoughts, feelings, or actions to be okay. In almost all situations, a huge middle ground exists.

4. **Overgeneralization:** You exaggerate negative experiences (anticipating the worst) and make faulty generalizations based on one experience. One bland Mexican meal does not mean *all* Mexican restaurants use only mild sauces.

5. **Mind Reading:** You presume to know what other people are thinking or feeling (without asking) and tend to assume they're focused on what's wrong with you or your work.

6. **Magnifying/Minimizing:** You make one minor problem a massive problem; slight obstacles become insurmountable roadblocks. You also *minimize* positive aspects of situations, thereby missing the good.

7. **Personalization:** You assume everything is about you, relying on others to determine *your* worthiness.

8. **Fortune Telling:** You forecast results based on little to no evidence, responding to "just a feeling" (emotional reasoning) or on what you *imagine* might happen.

9. **Blaming:** Rather than self-reflect, you blame others whenever possible.

10. **Shoulds:** You've created expectations on how one *should* behave, and your standards are almost always too high.

5-Minute Thought Stopping

To reduce distorted thinking, understanding how to stop the faulty thinking will help you learn to think more positively and logically. Simply pause long enough to:

- Identify the pattern of distorted thinking.
- Identify the distorted thought(s).
- Question its validity.
- Replace it with a realistic thought.

This is another form of cognitive behavioral therapy (CBT, see page 87) that will help you break negative thinking patterns.

FESS UP TO YOUR FAULTY THINKING

The first step in disrupting faulty thinking is to become aware of when you're doing it. Let's see how you do in identifying how your distorted thinking manifests. Spend five minutes on each manner of faulty thinking over the next few pages, pondering them carefully.

Write about a time you catastrophized. What were your most disturbing thoughts?

_____

_____

_____

_____

_____

_____

_____

_____

_____

_____

_____

_____

_____

_____

_____

_____

_____

_____

Were your thoughts valid? Did you realize that at the time? What caused you to leap to outlandish projections of a "worst-case" scenario? Is this way of thinking helpful?

_____

_____

_____

_____

_____

How did you cope? Were you able to corral and redirect your thoughts?

_____

_____

_____

_____

_____

Think of a possible situation in which you'd catastrophize. Write down your worst thoughts.

_____

_____

_____

_____

_____

Now, write down all the coping mechanisms you have and write about how resourceful you could be, if needed.

_____

_____

_____

_____

_____

_____

_____

Now, replace the catastrophic fears with realistic thoughts about what's likely to happen.

_____

_____

_____

_____

_____

_____

_____

TIP

To combat catastrophizing, avoid "what if" thinking or jumping to the worst conclusions. Challenge your distorted thoughts, replace them with realistic assessments, then list ways you'll be able to cope.

Write about a time you relied on filtered thinking. What did you blow out of proportion by focusing on the negative? Do you know why?

_____

_____

_____

_____

_____

_____

_____

What did you miss that was good? Can you give yourself credit for the good?

_____

_____

_____

_____

_____

_____

_____

TIP To combat filtering, keep your focus on the *solution* rather than the problem. Also, focus on the positive aspects, and keep any negatives in proper proportion.

Write about a time you relied on black and white thinking. What happened?

_____

_____

_____

_____

_____

_____

_____

_____

_____

_____

Do you typically think this way? Do you know when it started and why?

_____

_____

_____

_____

_____

_____

_____

_____

_____

_____

_____

_____

TIP

To combat black and white thinking, identify shades of gray. See if you can come up with ten shades of gray and/or assign a reality-based percentage somewhere in the middle.

What would be the middle ground in that situation?

_____

_____

_____

_____

_____

_____

How can you modify your way of thinking to avoid black and white thinking?

_____

_____

_____

_____

_____

_____

_____

Do you tend to overgeneralize? How does that occur? Does it reoccur in any areas of your life?

_____

_____

_____

_____

_____

_____

_____

_____

_____

_____

Do you see the faulty reasoning behind this type of thinking?

_____

_____

_____

_____

_____

_____

_____

_____

_____

_____

How can you avoid overgeneralizing in the future? What's a more flexible way of thinking?

_____

_____

_____

_____

_____

_____

Take a problem or task you face now and write about how you can defeat over-generalized thinking and then realistically identify and directly address the specifics of the problem.

_____

_____

_____

_____

_____

_____

_____

TIP

To combat overgeneralization, try to avoid exaggeration and rather than quantify a negative thought, be specific. Rather than saying, "Every time I try to complete a project on time, I fail miserably," say, "The last three times I handed the project in late, but I've since mastered time management and have every expectation that I'll complete my next project on time."

Do you practice mind reading, imagining that you know what other people are thinking, without checking with them to see if you're right? When are you most likely to do this?

_____

_____

_____

_____

_____

_____

_____

_____

When it happens do you envision that coworkers or contemporaries are having negative thoughts about you? Why do you jump to that conclusion?

_____

_____

_____

_____

_____

_____

_____

_____

_____

To combat mind reading, take people at their word, until they prove otherwise. Also, if you can't outright ask them what they're thinking (or feeling), imagine five neutral possibilities and accept that these are more likely true.

What prevents you from asking people what they're thinking? Identify any fears behind the failure to ask. What do you think others really think about your abilities?

_____

_____

_____

_____

_____

_____

_____

_____

_____

_____

_____

_____

_____

_____

_____

_____

_____

Do you magnify negative thoughts and minimize positive ones? Think about a time you last did so and write about it. What happened and how did your thoughts turn a small obstacle into a major roadblock?

_____

_____

_____

_____

_____

_____

_____

_____

_____

Were your thoughts valid? Did your worst thoughts come true?

_____

_____

_____

_____

_____

_____

_____

_____

_____

_____

Did you miss something positive? Write down all the positive comments you have received about your work or ability to execute necessary tasks. What do you really know about your efficacy?

_____

_____

_____

_____

_____

_____

_____

_____

_____

_____

_____

_____

_____

_____

_____

_____

TIP

To combat magnifying, downgrade your adjectives (avoid extreme assessments) and expectations (worst fears). Acknowledge obstacles as something you have the resources to overcome. To avoid minimizing the good, make sure you always identify the good in every situation.

Do you tend to personalize most things by assuming anything negative is ultimately about you?

_____

_____

_____

_____

_____

_____

_____

_____

Why did you make those assumptions? Do you feel insecure about your abilities? Your looks? Your personality?

_____

_____

_____

_____

_____

_____

_____

_____

_____

What makes you feel most vulnerable to perceived criticism?

_____

_____

_____

_____

_____

Are those assessments accurate? Write statements that counteract them.

_____

_____

_____

_____

_____

_____

Do you often worry about what other people think about you? In what area of your life is this most concerning?

_____

_____

_____

_____

_____

_____

Why do you imagine others to be so critical? Is this realistic? Spend five minutes writing about the genesis of your irrational fears about criticism. Once you see where they began, you can learn to let them go.

_____

_____

_____

_____

_____

_____

_____

_____

_____

_____

_____

_____

_____

_____

_____

_____

TIP

To combat personalization, assume that no one is judging you, until proven otherwise. Focus on your own thoughts about yourself. Don't assume you have power to affect other people's moods.

Do you practice fortune-telling, imagining what will happen without basing your conclusions on evidence?

_____

_____

_____

_____

_____

_____

Do you see how you might be basing your focused, specific-to-the-situation thinking on emotional reasoning or irrational justifications, feeling rather than thinking?

_____

_____

_____

_____

_____

_____

TIP To combat fortune-telling, instead of allowing fear to fog your thinking, use valid evidence and rational reasoning to forecast results.

When something goes wrong, do you immediately look for someone else to blame? Are you aware of this tendency? Do you have difficulty accepting responsibility for even minor mistakes?

_____

_____

_____

_____

_____

_____

_____

_____

Are you fearful of being scrutinized? When might that fear arise? Can you identify your fears and their common triggers?

_____

_____

_____

_____

_____

_____

_____

_____

Can you remember the last time you blamed someone else? Was it fair? What were you trying to avoid? What do you think would happen if you accept full responsibility in the future?

_____

_____

_____

_____

_____

_____

_____

_____

_____

_____

_____

_____

_____

_____

_____

_____

_____

TIP To combat blaming, pause before pointing the finger at anyone or any situation. First, self-reflect, then focus your thoughts and discuss the problem in terms of solutions.

What are your shoulds*? Make a list of rules you tend to hold fast to.*

_____

_____

_____

_____

_____

_____

Do you hold everyone to the same shoulds?

_____

_____

_____

_____

_____

_____

Are these shoulds realistic?

_____

_____

_____

_____

_____

_____

Think of 3 exceptions for every should you listed.

_____

_____

_____

_____

_____

_____

_____

_____

_____

_____

What would be the middle ground on your shoulds?

_____

_____

_____

_____

_____

_____

_____

_____

_____

_____

_____

Can you adopt a more flexible attitude? What do you think would happen if you relaxed your standards?

_____

_____

_____

_____

_____

_____

_____

_____

_____

_____

_____

_____

_____

_____

_____

_____

_____

_____

TIP

To combat shoulds, examine your tendency to use words like "should," "must," "have to," "ought," and replace them with "prefer." Moderate a tendency to hold everyone (especially yourself) to exacting standards.

To learn to think

is to learn how to live.

Dan Custer, *The Miracle of Mind Power*

One of the most persistent

of all delusions is the conviction

that the source of our dissatisfaction

lies outside ourselves.

Alan Wallace, *Buddhist author*

Switch to
Positive, Productive Thinking

In *The Art of Thinking*, authors Allen Harrison and Robert Bramson identified five styles of productive thinking and said knowing which styles you tend to use helps you learn to utilize your thinking patterns—and try new ones. Utilizing more than one style is preferable, and it's always good to try something that feels out of character. The five thinking styles are:

1. **Synthesists** tend to enjoy conflict and challenging authority. You love playing devil's advocate and proffering "what if" questions. Challenge and *what if*s are good, but you use conflict to fuel your creativity and can benefit from seeing the whole picture.

2. **Idealists** more often look at the whole of a picture rather than just one component. You are more interested in people and feelings than facts and numbers. You enjoy thinking and making plans, particularly for their future. You need more grounding.

3. **Pragmatists** prefer to do "whatever works." You are a quick thinker who does well with short-term planning. You are often creative and quite adaptable to change. You may be comfortable doing things "on the fly" without any sort of plan whatsoever. Maybe pause occasionally to think creatively.

4. **Analysts** tend to try to break down a problem into its specific components rather than dealing with it as a whole. You make lists, organize things, and rely on detail, in hopes you can keep your life and problems orderly. You may be too focused on the minor details.

5. **Realists** ask tough questions, take a no-nonsense approach to problems, and tend to do whatever is necessary to achieve a solution. You have a solid grasp on the problem at hand and the tools with which you can solve it. You also know your limitations. Most people have some realist aspects. But a little idealism and flexibility are also good.

So, what type of thinking style do you rely on? Can you identify two others that you often use? Take five minutes to think about a current problem you have and write about how you might employ each style of thinking to come up with solutions.

1. _____

_____

2. _____

_____

3. _____

_____

4. _____

_____

5. _____

_____

5-Minute Brain Boosters

Thinking is a deliberate process and just like any muscle in your body, the more you think, the better you'll be able to think. Here are six ways to bolster your brain's thinking abilities:

1. Bolster your math skills by not always reaching for a calculator—buy yourself a math workbook instead.
2. Do crossword puzzles or other word games to build your vocabulary and improve memory.
3. Memorize a poem to strengthen active memory. You can also memorize interesting facts or quotes to use in conversation.
4. Learn something new as often as possible. Read books you don't normally read, study subjects that befuddle you—look for ways to open, surprise, and delight your mind.
5. Challenge your brain by not using GPS and taking new routes in your area, watching a documentary on something you know nothing about, learning a new word, trying a new sport, painting or drawing, practicing a foreign language, or volunteering.
6. Stay curious. Curious people tend to be smart people who gather a lot of interesting information about the world, which then helps them think better when facing new challenges.

To maximize your brain's capacity to think, flex those thinking muscles five minutes a day.

PRACTICE DIVERGENT THINKING

Practice *divergent* thinking rather than convergent thinking. Convergent thinking is when you only see two choices (we can win, or we can lose; people are either good or bad). Divergent thinking means opening your mind in all directions (realizing that options and people are complex, with elements of good, bad, indifferent, and everything in between).

To use more divergent thinking, whenever you encounter people or a situation, pay attention to how you're framing the situation or person. Are you only seeing limited options? Or are you allowing your thinking to expand and envision multiple, more complex options?

_____

_____

_____

_____

_____

_____

_____

_____

_____

_____

_____

_____

Now that you've learned techniques for improving the way your brain thinks, let's discuss how to train your brain to pay closer attention. Paying attention is crucial to productivity.

Take up one idea.

Make that one idea your life:

think of it,

dream of it,

live on that idea.

Let the brain, muscles, nerves, every part of your body, be full of that idea, and just leave every other idea alone.

This is the way to success.

Swami Vivekananda, *philosopher*

CHAPTER 5

Improve Your Brain's Ability to Pay Attention

"Attention must not only be focused for us to take action, but it must also be receptive so we can notice and observe what is occurring before us (in the moment)."

Amisha P. Jha, Ph.D., *Peak Mind*

Given the modern, interconnected, fast-paced world we live in, keeping our minds fully focused on what we need to do is often challenging. We have far too many tasks on our daily lists, far too many needs to juggle in our lives, and a lot of worries on our minds. With cell phones ringing, texts clicking in, and email notifications and DMs pinging, we often feel simultaneously pulled in multiple directions, required to constantly shift our attention. It's small wonder that learning to focus our thoughts and better manage our minds have become paramount to productivity. Many are turning to the Buddhist practice of meditation, and particularly mindfulness meditation, to train their brains to pay attention to what is happening in the moment.

According to Dr. Amisha P. Jha, author of *Peak Mind*, during mindfulness practice and meditation, the brain networks tied to focusing and managing attention, noticing and monitoring internal and external events, and mind wandering are all activated. Over time, Dr. Jha writes, mindfulness strengthens key nodes in the network that are tied to your brain's ability to pay attention, improves connection between the area that handles attention and your default mode (rote thinking), and tamps down default mode activity.

Jump on the
Mindfulness Bandwagon

Quite simply, mindfulness is cultivating awareness on what is happening in the present moment, without relying on past experiences or your usual way of thinking and reacting. It's the art of focusing your brain's full attention on what you're doing in the immediate present, without allowing thoughts about the past or the future to interfere.

If you were cooking, for example, being mindful would mean that you keep your focus on how it feels to slice the onion, how the onion smells, feels, tastes, burns your eyes, how the knife feels slicing through it, and the sound of the slices landing on the cutting board. In other words, it's not allowing any outside stimuli (or previous thoughts about onions) to interfere with exactly what you're doing. As you can imagine, this is a useful skill to learn.

The mind is just like a muscle—

the more you exercise it,

the stronger it gets,

and the more it can expand.

Idowu Koyenikan, *author*

5-MINUTE MINDFULNESS MEDITATION

There are only a few things required to mindfully meditate.

Ideally, you'll find a quiet, private space where you can sit upright, with a straight spine, for 3 to 5 minutes. You may want to set a timer.

Sit comfortably and upright to align your spine, sitting either cross-legged on the floor or in a chair with your feet flat on the floor (to ground yourself). Once settled, breathe in and out, slowly, deeply, drawing the breaths into your lungs and down to your belly, then slowly releasing them from your belly. Keep breathing, focusing solely on your breath, until you can successfully bring your attention to your breath, and only your breath.

Dismiss all arising thoughts that interfere with the sole focus on your breath. Instead, concentrate on how your breath feels going slowly in and slowly out, how warm it feels, how comforting and restorative it feels, and how grateful you are to have beautifully functioning lungs, while concurrently dismissing all other thoughts. They will pop up repeatedly, trying desperately to grab your attention. Your job is to send them sailing off into the stratosphere.

If you have difficulty solely focusing on what's happening in the moment, you can use a mantra (a phrase that calms and comforts you) or an object, such as a candle, to focus on. If necessary, you can keep saying or thinking: "I'm here, breathing slowly, in and out" or "I am focused solely on my breath" over and over.

Every time you notice your mind wandering, practice bringing it back to what needs your attention.

You can find a wealth of mindfulness meditation websites online, and many are free, such as The Free Mindfulness Project (http://freemindfulness.org).

Listen to silence,

it has much to say.

Rumi

Write about your mindfulness meditation. What did you find difficult about sitting still, focused solely on your breathing? Were you able to quiet your thoughts? Release them as soon as they appeared?

_____

_____

_____

_____

_____

_____

_____

_____

_____

_____

_____

_____

_____

_____

_____

_____

_____

_____

_____

_____

_____

_____

_____

Attention Booster

Neuroscientific studies have shown that mindfulness meditation has many benefits, such as improving:

- function of your anterior cingulate cortex, which boosts self-regulation, the ability to purposefully direct attention and seamlessly switch strategies;
- function in your hippocampus, which helps with stress reduction, emotional balance, improved outlook, and memory;
- cognitive control (focus), introspection, and complex thinking.

Other studies have shown that monks and nuns who regularly mindfully meditate were *significantly* more adept at concentration and paying attention, while simultaneously reducing the sort of "me" thinking that distracts the brain from the task at hand.

According to the Pew Research Center, **40%** of Americans meditate at least once a week...and **45%** rarely or never do.

Improve Time, Improve Focus

To obtain long-term mindfulness meditation results, you may want to try meditating regularly, increasing the amount of time to up to 30 minutes a session. Once you're an accomplished meditator (somewhere between 10 and 15 minutes has been identified as ideal), you can always do five-minute meditations whenever needed, as they will calm and focus your brain.

TIP

Best Meditation Apps

Best Overall: Calm
Best Budget Service: Ten Percent Happier Meditation
Best Guided Meditation: Core Meditation
Best Audio Selection: Headspace
Best for Beginners: Waking Up
Best for Short Sessions: The Mindfulness App
Best Free Service: Insight Timer
Best for Mindfulness: Simple Habit Sleep
Best for Mantras: Sattva Meditations & Mantras

(Source: Goodhousekeeping.com)

Ground Yourself
in the Moment

If you feel stressed or fearful, your brain will likely go into "fight or flight" mode, which takes all awareness out of your body and into your "reptile brain," the one solely focused on survival. Unless the situation requires you to fight or flee, taking five minutes to focus on restoring body awareness will both calm you and help your "thinking brain" focus on solutions.

Stress is basically a disconnection

from the earth,

a forgetting of the breath.

Nothing is that important.

Just lie down.

Natalie Goldberg, *Zen author*

5-MINUTE GROUNDING MEDITATION

Bringing awareness to your body within your current surroundings by drawing your full attention to how your body feels helps ground you in the moment. Get into position (see page 137), breathe in and out slowly, then open your eyes, but keep your gaze low. Slowly scan your surroundings, keeping your focus on how your body feels in its current situation. Take note of what is happening around you, without lifting your gaze, and assess whether it's truly threatening or if your anxiety is out of proportion to what is really happening.

Be aware of how your body feels as you make this assessment, and breathe into the feelings, releasing those that caused the anxiety and breathing in peace. Cross your hands over your heart and feel its strength.

Take five minutes to write about your grounding meditation. Did you feel more grounded in your body, in the present moment? Were you able to release the angry or upsetting emotions? Did it help shift focus from your emotions to clarity on solutions?

_____

_____

_____

_____

_____

_____

_____

_____

_____

_____

_____

_____

5-Minute Creativity

If you need a creative solution, here are thought-provoking questions to ask yourself:

1. If you had access to all needed resources, how would you do this?
2. If you could ask anyone, who would you ask to help you?
3. If you weren't afraid of failure, what would you try?

Rather than getting stuck on limitations, these questions help you see greater possibilities.

Improve Focus Via a Gyan Mudra

Ever feel so rattled you can't think? Buddhists believe in the sacred positioning of fingers to guide the flow of energy in meditation, and scientists have confirmed that learned hand gestures activate the same brain regions as written or spoken words. The next time you feel so anxious and unsettled you can't think, try a focusing meditation.

5-MINUTE FOCUSING MEDITATION

Begin by breathing in and out slowly, then rest your hands, palm up, on your lap. Touch the tips of your thumbs to tips of your index fingers, forming a circle, while extending your other fingers until they are straight. Buddhists consider the thumb representational of the universe's soul and the finger your soul. Touching them together is thought to bring a union of those two energies, which helps clear your mind, improve alertness, and enhance clarity. Spend five minutes, eyes closed, breathing in and out, holding the *gyan mudra* position. Imagine yourself connected to the universe and ask for clarity, focus, energy, peace, or whatever you need in the moment.

If you want to go quickly, *go alone.*

If you want to go far, *go together.*

African proverb

Write about your gyan mudra meditation. Did you discover something about yourself? Something you want or need to feel more comfortable? Were you able to envision a connection to the universe?

_____

_____

_____

_____

_____

_____

_____

_____

_____

_____

_____

_____

_____

_____

_____

_____

_____

_____

_____

_____

_____

_____

5-Minute See-It-and-Believe-It Meditation

If you are facing a challenging task, try a simulation meditation. Once you're relaxed and focused on your breathing, envision the successful outcome of your challenge. See yourself moments after you've successfully accomplished the task. Try to both see and *feel* how success will look and feel. The more deeply you can create the future scenario, the more likely your brain is to believe it's already true. This can streamline the path from conception to completion as your brain has effectively "seen" the way forward.

Alleviate Conflict Via a
Metta Kindness Meditation

> "A single act of kindness throws out roots in all directions, and roots spring up and make new trees."
> Amelia Earhart, *aviator*

Ever notice how relationship friction can make it extremely hard to focus? The Buddha encouraged all humans, but particularly those feeling conflict, to practice a metta kindness meditation.

5-MINUTE METTA KINDNESS MEDITATION

Simply bring yourself to your normal meditative state, then focus on making a series of loving statements, such as: "May I be happy and free from suffering." Take in the good wishes for yourself. Now, think of someone you respect and offer them the same blessings. Then, think of a dear friend and send them loving wishes. Then, think of a neutral figure (your UPS delivery person, perhaps) and send them loving kindness. Then, think of the person causing your current distress, and send them loving kindness. Then, send loving kindness out to all beings. If you find it hard to think of the person causing your conflict, try saying the words gently; but don't force false feelings. In time, you'll learn how to lovingly accept and forgive someone, even when you are angry about their behavior. This will make it easier to collaborate.

Write about your metta meditation. If you couldn't exactly feel love for the person causing you distress, were you able to release your anger? Do you feel like you can be more patient and forgiving when frustrated? What would you ask for yourself in a future metta kindness meditation?

_____

_____

_____

_____

_____

_____

_____

_____

_____

_____

_____

_____

_____

_____

_____

_____

_____

_____

_____

_____

_____

_____

_____

Metta Really Delivers

The Buddha promised marvelous results from practicing loving kindness, metta meditation. He said:

You will sleep easily.

You will wake easily.

You will have pleasant dreams.

People will love you.

Devas (celestial beings) will love and protect you.

Your mind will be serene.

He also promised you'd die happy, so that seems worth a few metta meditations.

TIP

Here are some other phrases for your metta kindness meditation:
"May I/you be safe."
"May I/you be healthy."
"May I/you be strong and confident."
"May my/your mind be at ease."
"May I/you be gentle with myself/yourself."

Improve Focus with a
Kirtan Kriya Meditation

The Alzheimer's Research Association found that *kirtan kriya* meditation has positive effects on the brain, including:

→ Improved blood flow to the cerebral cortex, which improves thinking.

→ Improved blood flow to the posterior cingulate gyrus, which improves memory retrieval.

→ Increased activity in the frontal lobe, which sharpens attention, focus, and concentration.

→ Replenishment of vital neurotransmitters, which helps the brain work more smoothly.

→ Increased energy levels and reduced cortisol, which reduces stress.

In other words, it primes your brain for the kind of productive thinking you hope to achieve.

Accentuate the Positive

In even dire situations, positives exist. They're just drowned out by your brain's focus on what's causing fear or anxiety. When you are consumed by negative thoughts or emotions, stop, breathe slowly in and out until you feel calmer, then notice and preferably write down a list of positives that are also happening. The more you focus on the positives, the sooner a solution to your dilemma may "magically" appear.

5-MINUTE KIRTAN KRIYA MEDITATION

Once you have your breath slowed down, place your hands,
palm-up, on your lap (or hold them in the air if you like).

Begin by softly chanting "Saa, Taa, Naa, Maa."

Touch your index fingertip to your thumb tip as you say "Saa,"
then release it and touch your middle fingertip to your thumb as you say "Taa,"
"Naa" to your ring finger, and "Maa" to your little finger.

The coordination of sound and touch activate motor and sensory areas of your brain and your occipital lobe, which can help you have clarity of purpose and a "vision" of what you need to do.

As you continue the coordinated chanting and fingertip touching, envision energy coming down from the crown of your head to your third eye, the site of intuition (located just between your eyes), then send the energy directly out to the universe (envision the area between your eyes as the foot of an "L" that proceeds up and out the top of your head to direct the energy up and out). If you are alone, singing the chant and increasing the volume of your singing can further assist. When ready, lay your hands on your lap and slow your breathing until you are ready to end your meditation. Take advantage of your fired up brain.

TIP
If you notice procrastination or anxiety affecting your focus, taking five minutes to do a *kirtan kirya* meditation is an effective way to focus your frontal cortex. Start slow and chant in your mind, if necessary, then gradually increase your touching speed for three minutes, then gradually slow it back down.

Write about your kirtan kriya meditation. How did this meditation feel? Did you have trouble with coordination? Did you feel as if it helped focus your brain? Do you see how even a few minutes of focused finger/word connection could help you stop nonproductive thoughts and refocus on the task? Identify situations in which a kirtan kriya focusing meditation could truly benefit your thought process.

_____

_____

_____

_____

_____

_____

_____

_____

_____

_____

_____

_____

_____

_____

_____

_____

_____

Learning methods to think and pay attention more effectively will help you boost everyday productivity in countless ways. Let's move to discuss practical solutions to handle the distractions that typically limit productivity.

CHAPTER 6

Practical Solutions

> "If I were dropped out of a plane into the ocean and told the nearest land was a thousand miles away, I'd still swim. And I'd despise the one who gave up."
> Abraham Maslow, *social psychologist*

Psychologist Abraham Maslow formulated a hierarchy of needs that he believed all humans share. Usually represented by a triangle, the needs at the base are centered on staying alive and reproducing (food, sex, sleep, homeostasis); the second level up focuses on safety and security (a place to live, employment, family, health, resources); the third level is about love and belonging (friendship, family, sexual intimacy, connection); the fourth level is about self-esteem (confidence, achievement, respect of others, respect by others); and the fifth is self-actualization (morality, creativity, spontaneity, problem-solving, lack of prejudice, acceptance of facts). Maslow postulated that all your other needs must be met before you can reach self-actualization.

The drive for self-actualization reflects the desire for self-fulfillment, or a person's drive to become more fully who they are.

SELF-ACTUALIZATION
desire to become the most that one can be

ESTEEM
respect, self-esteem, status, recognition, strength, freedom

LOVE AND BELONGING
friendship, intimacy, family, sense of connection

SAFETY NEEDS
personal security, employment, resources, health, property

PHYSIOLOGICAL NEEDS
air, water, food, shelter, sleep, clothing, reproduction

Why You Want to Self-Actualize

According to Abraham Maslow, the psychological theorist who helped define it, self-actualized people tend to be:

- Integrated, true to themselves, and trusting of themselves.
- Independent and resourceful, without the need for anyone to direct their lives.
- Creative, resourceful, adventurous, and spontaneous.
- Empathetic, moral, and caring about others' well-being.
- Capable of deep and loving relationships with others.
- Accepting of their own and others' flaws.
- Adaptable, able to go through life with ease, and able to lighten up and laugh easily.
- Grateful, holding a deep appreciation for small blessings.
- Able to tell what's superficial from what's real when judging situations.
- Knowing of themselves, forming their own opinions based on their perceptions.

Becoming self-actualized represents the pinnacle of living. You would be your best self and genuinely happy.

Obviously, a self-actualized person is a fully integrated personality (he is who he is, and he stands fully in who he is), and the consistency, confidence, and self-assurance that comes with being self-actualized means that you'd be operating at peak performance. But all of us must contend with our hierarchy of needs, which means practical strategies for doing what must be done to make us more productive are essential to our very existence.

Let's work on bolstering organizational skills designed to boost your productivity.

Establish Goals
for Each Day, Week, Month

We discussed creating major life goals earlier, but it is also extremely productive to create goals for each day, week, month, even year. Doing so gives your brain something to focus on, often while you are busy doing something else. Goals also help you focus when "on task" and feel accomplishment as you check each completed task. Again, when setting goals, be specific, be positive, and be realistic (make them achievable within the timeframe you set).

While the dreamers

are still sleeping,

the doers

are taking victory laps.

Linda Kaplan Thaler and Robin Koval,
Grit to Great

TIP
When you create goals, you are envisioning a successful future. To help your brain truly "see" them as achievable (and already a reality), use positive language. Instead of, "I will stop chatting with my mother while at work," change it to, "I will focus while at work and call my mother in the evening."

Take five minutes to contemplate, then write down your five major goals for the month. If you have more, feel free to extend the list.

1. _____

2. _____

3. _____

4. _____

5. _____

Strike off any goals that you cannot achieve in one month. Perhaps break the unachievable goal down to something you can do that works toward it.

_____

_____

_____

_____

_____

_____

_____

_____

_____

_____

Now, take another five minutes to identify ten smaller, more specific goals for this week. Set a deadline for getting each done.

1. _____

   Deadline: _____

2. _____

   Deadline: _____

3. _____

   Deadline: _____

4. _____

   Deadline: _____

5. _____

   Deadline: _____

6. _____

   Deadline: _____

7. _____

   Deadline: _____

8. _____

   Deadline: _____

9. _____

   Deadline: _____

10. _____

   Deadline: _____

Strike off any goals that you cannot realistically achieve in one week or break each down to what you can achieve. Narrow your focus to what you can *succeed* at doing, and set a deadline for each achievable goal.

Now, taking your list of goals for the week in mind, what are your specific goals for tomorrow?

1.
_____
Deadline:

2.
_____
Deadline:

3.
_____
Deadline:

4.
_____
Deadline:

5.
_____
Deadline:

Strike off what you cannot get done in one day and commit to what you can achieve. Set the deadline that it will be completed in one day.

TIP   Write down what you need to get accomplished. Research shows that writing down your "to-do" list and schedule for the day makes you feel more engaged in the task at hand. And neuroscience backs this up by finding that vividly writing down goals encodes them in your brain, which makes you more likely to achieve them.

Put Your Overnight Brain to Work

When you face a challenge, spend time the night before writing about it. Spend five minutes writing down the specifics, focusing on the challenge, and then ask your inventive brain to think about solutions while you sleep. While your conscious self sleeps, your brain processes everything that happened that day. If you practice this regularly, your clever brain will get in the habit of generating ideas to help.

GOALS VERSUS TASKS

Tasks are a series of "to do" items that move you closer to achieving a short-term goal. A short-term goal is a bar you set for yourself that achieves something of value. Goals should be:

→ **Specific:** Use specific, positive language to describe what you want to achieve.

→ **Measurable:** You need quantifiable results in a set amount of time.

→ **Attainable:** A bit of stretch is okay, but it should be doable within the set amount of time.

→ **Valuable:** It should align with your core values.

→ **Progressive:** Achievement should be a step toward a long-term goal.

→ **Primary:** A top priority that will motivate you to be productive.

Remember to set a deadline for each goal and task and to hold yourself accountable for meeting them. If you fall short, you set your goals too high. Give yourself credit for learning to set goals and keep moving forward.

The following page has an exercise for how to break down goals into manageable tasks. This is a method you can use each day to bolster productivity. Everything is easier to do if broken down into easily achievable tasks.

TIP

Kanban is a simple but effective project management technique. All you need are some sticky notes and a whiteboard with three columns labeled "To-do," "In progress," and "Done." By moving the sticky notes left to right across the board, you can visualize how efficiently you're completing tasks while maintaining an overview of your other responsibilities.

Choose your top five goals for the week and spend five minutes breaking each down into "doable chunks."

1. a. _____

    b. _____

    c. _____

    d. _____

    e. _____

2. a. _____

    b. _____

    c. _____

    d. _____

    e. _____

3. a. _____

    b. _____

    c. _____

    d. _____

    e. _____

4. a. _____

    b. _____

    c. _____

    d. _____

    e. _____

5. a. _____

    b. _____

    c. _____

    d. _____

    e. _____

Practice Single Tasking

Most people think multitasking is a fabulous way to boost productivity, but they would be wrong. Your brain cannot simultaneously do two activities that require *cognitive attention*. When you attempt two activities that require your prefrontal (thinking) cortex, it must repeatedly shift from one task to the other. In fact, according to a French study, the two areas of your brain trying to multitask begin competing against each other, rather than working together. It's best to marshal all your brain resources on one task at a time.

Mothers can nurse their baby and read a legal brief at the same time, because only one task requires cognition. You can also listen to music while working—if the volume remains low and consistent. Changes in stimuli distract your brain, as will switching from reading on your cell phone to reading on your computer. It's also why you turn down the radio when traffic requires your attention. Brains need time to shift and a single task to focus on. *Estimates suggest that productivity can be reduced by as much as 40 percent when constantly switching between tasks.*

CHECK OFF YOUR SUCCESSES

Get in the habit of writing a "to do" list of the doable chunks each day. As you accomplish each task, check it off, and pause to feel proud that you've achieved the kind of productivity you desire. When you completed all the doable chunks and each daily goal is met, *reward yourself*. It can be as simple as buying yourself a sparkling water or taking five minutes to meditate. Every time you reward yourself, you are reinforcing productive action. The more often you practice goal setting, the better you'll get at creating achievable goals and meeting them. Over time, this can dramatically boost your productivity and your confidence.

To bolster productivity, create a daily action plan. Spend five minutes at the beginning of each day to write down your intentions for what you plan to achieve that day (or for a period of hours). If necessary, break it down into tasks, then prioritize tasks you want to accomplish and set a deadline for getting each task done. Keep your action plan focused and simple and use the list to check off your progress. If you're falling short on your daily action plans, pare them down. If you're excelling, boost them a little.

Spend five minutes at the beginning of your day to write down what you plan to achieve. You can replicate this exercise in a journal or notebook, or even on your computer.

_____

_____

_____

_____

_____

_____

TIP   Planners remain a great way to get your life organized. You can find a wealth of options to choose from, both print and digital, so shop around for one that works with your sensibilities and learn how to use it effectively.

Another useful exercise is to prioritize the list of doable chunks. Take a goal you set for one day and identify which doable chunk needs to be done first, second, third. Give yourself a deadline, such as: Task #1 will be done by 11 a.m.; Task #2 by 2 p.m.; Task #3 by 5 p.m.

Task #1   Deadline:

1.

2.

3.

4.

5.

Task #2   Deadline:

1.

2.

3.

4.

5.

Task #3   Deadline:

1.

2.

3.

4.

5.

Love Your Deadlines

Deadlines or benchmarks are excellent ways to hold yourself accountable and to take your plans from the idea stage to the action stage. The more specific you are about what you want, when you want it, and what you're willing to do to achieve it, the more productive you'll be. Without deadlines, you are far more likely to put things off; and without benchmarks, you're missing opportunities to track your progress, celebrate, and reinforce your ability to march forward toward your goals.

Create a Brain Storm

Brainstorming (mind mapping) is a productive way to gather your thoughts. Whether you use drawn balloons or simple lines to connect offshoot ideas, doing so sparks neuronal connections. The mental and visual act also focuses your brain on any memories or skills it has stored related to that task, creating a new, heightened cluster of neuronal connections. The deeper you dive, the greater the brain *storms* those neuronal connections generate.

Establish Boundaries

Remove anything and everything that bogs down, limits, or prevents your success. This may include a work environment where you are constantly interrupted, or one where your best efforts are repeatedly subverted. It also includes abusive relationships that diminish your self-esteem, or coworkers or family members who don't value your time. Obviously, it's not desirable to simply banish people (well, some), but you can set boundaries that establish how much *you* value your time.

> "Boundary setting helps you prioritize your needs over someone else's wants."
> Lauren Kenson, *Free to Thrive* podcast

TIP To identify how you waste your time, spend five minutes every few hours noticing when and how you procrastinated. See if you can identify what precipitated slacking off. Just don't spend so much time reflecting that it turns into yet another way to procrastinate.

DON'T LET ANYONE DISRUPT YOUR FLOW

Spend five minutes making a list of at least 5 situations in which you need to set boundaries. Note that boundaries may need to be set around time spent reading news online, scrolling through all your emails before getting to work, responding to IMs, chatting with coworkers, or saying "no" to projects you cannot take on.

1. _____

_____

2. _____

_____

3. _____

_____

4. _____

_____

5. _____

_____

Talent is cheaper than table salt.
What separates the *talented individual*
from the *successful one*
is a lot of *hard work.*

Stephen King, *author*

Describe how you will establish boundaries for the five situations you identified.
Ideas might be to set a timer, respond only to "top priority emails," or block off
two hours each day during which nothing (neither DMs nor a frustrated coworker
or spouse) is allowed to interrupt you.

1. _____

_____

_____

2. _____

_____

_____

3. _____

_____

_____

4. _____

_____

_____

5. _____

_____

_____

Vigilantly reinforce your boundaries. Write about any continuing problems and how you can address them.

_____

_____

_____

_____

_____

_____

_____

_____

_____

_____

_____

_____

_____

_____

Make a "To Do" List for Your Life

We often procrastinate when we feel stressed, and often that stress comes from a multitude of demands—at work and at home. Figure out what's left undone at home that's bugging you at work and either make a "To Do" list of the items to address later or go ahead and strike a few items off that list right now. You're effectively externalizing your thoughts, which frees your distracted mind so it can focus.

DEFEAT ENEMIES OF THE PRESENT

The more you live in the present, as opposed to the ruminating about the past or forecasting into the future, the more focused and productive you'll be. Things that make remaining *fully present* in the here and now difficult are:

1. Projecting your thoughts backward into what happened in the past or forward into what you imagine might happen in the future. Both pull you away from the present moment.
2. Allowing yourself to be distracted. The more you focus your full attention on doing one thing at a time, the more fully present you'll be. That means turning off your phone when you really need to be present.
3. Feeling fatigued makes it hard to bring everything you've got to whatever is happening in the present moment. Rushing around to do too many things has a similar effect.
4. Being impatient for things to happen takes away from what *is* happening, in the present. It's best to allow life to unfold and enjoy the ride, as it happens.
5. Analyzing what's happening while it's happening distracts you from the experience itself. We all tend to overthink these days. Often, it's best to simply observe what *is* and accept the experience.

Being fully present in the moment increases awareness and enjoyment. It also helps you focus, which helps you be more productive.

Take five minutes to consider ways that you sabotage being fully in the present. Write down a strategy for being fully present, particularly when striving for productivity.

Take a 5-Minute Brain Vacation

Often when you've been concentrating for a long time, and particularly if you feel blocked, taking a short break to do something completely unrelated will shake things up enough to bolster productivity. Albert Einstein played the violin to pause focused thinking; Vladimir Nabokov collected and studied butterflies. Some people take a walk, or a shower, or look at art. If you can take time off from your workflow and let your mind wander—maybe doodle, listen to music, draw pictures, just stare out the window—those periods of inactivity will refresh your brain and lead to increased periods of productivity.

MAKE THE MOST OF EACH DAY

If you're not making the best use of each day, you're selling yourself short. Unfortunately, most of us fall prey to distractions that detract from the best use of our time. Some ways you might be distracted are:

→ Doing what's important to someone else rather than what's important to you.

→ Repeatedly postponing something you really want to do.

→ Waiting for the *perfect* opportunity to do something.

→ Sabotaging what is happening by focusing on negative feelings, such as worrying about something else, feeling resentful that it's not just the way you wanted it, feeling sad, being angry about something that's ultimately not important.

Take five minutes to explore the ways you sell yourself short.

_____

_____

_____

_____

_____

_____

_____

_____

_____

Take five minutes to ponder how can you make the most of each day.

_____

_____

_____

_____

_____

_____

_____

_____

_____

_____

Simplify *Your Life*

If you really want to bolster your productivity, simplifying your life is the surest way to go. The fewer possessions you have the less time you'll need to spend acquiring, organizing, tending to, cleaning, and eventually disposing of those possessions. The fewer activities you engage in the more time you free up for focusing on what you want to accomplish. It goes back to establishing your priorities in life. Here are some tips, ideas, and writing prompts to explore your priorities and time management.

 5-Minute Clutter Buster

Survey your surroundings and imagine eliminating 15 percent of your possessions in each room. Can you choose easily? Can you get as high as 25 percent? Make a list of everything you can easily move out of your living space, and make a plan to do so immediately. Do the same exercise in your workspace.

"When making the best decisions, we need to think about more than the 'yes' or the 'no.' We need to think about the 'why.'"
Linda Kaplan Thaler and Robin Koval,
Grit to Great

Given the new insights you have about your priorities, make a list of ten ways you could choose to immediately simplify your life (creating a leaner, more efficient workspace; hiring outside help; ordering in meals; cancelling social engagements; limiting social media browsing; limiting TV time).

1. _____

2. _____

3. _____

4. _____

5. _____

6. _____

7. _____

8. _____

9. _____

10. _____

Practice 5-Minute Prep Time
Whenever you have a task to do, spend five minutes gathering everything you'll need to complete it. Put all the materials in one, easily accessible spot. For tasks you do often, keep the necessary tools easily accessible all the time.

Pause to think about the time you just freed up for the coming week. Take five minutes to ponder how you'll make the best use of the newly freed-up time. Commit below to a certain amount of time focused on reaching goals, whether personal or professional.

_____

_____

_____

_____

_____

_____

_____

_____

_____

 5-Minute Efficiency Assessment

If you repeatedly face the same tasks, take five minutes to consider ways you can streamline the activities involved. Are all the tasks essential? Can you delegate? Can you ask for or hire help? Can you consolidate errands? Are you duplicating efforts? Is there software available that could make it easier, quicker? Thinking about *how* you fulfill your tasks may help you come up with ways to prioritize and be more efficient.

BE VIGILANT ABOUT HOW YOU SPEND YOUR TIME

Our time is our most valuable commodity, and nothing stops clocks from ticking forward. You might be surprised to learn that you, like a lot of people, waste 30 percent of your time on social media. Time to take stock.

🕐 5-Minute Taking Stock Task

Spend five minutes assessing how well you utilized your time in the past week. How much of that time did you waste? How much of that time was spent focused on your top priorities? Your weekly goals? Your life goals? Do you see nonproductive pattern? See if you can plan a way to maximize time in the week ahead. Commit to your plan on paper.

_____

_____

_____

_____

_____

_____

_____

_____

_____

_____

_____

_____

Ramp up Your Energy

Sleep is crucial. It's when your body, particularly your brain, restores, renews, and reorganizes itself. As your conscious self sleeps, your cells mend, your energy replenishes, your mood stabilizes, your brain repairs, and your health optimizes. To achieve maximum benefit, your body needs to sleep soundly 7 ½ to 9 hours a night.

Get Rich While You Sleep!
According to the Franklin Institute, an hour of extra sleep a night—the equivalent of a long nap—will boost your happiness comparable to a $60,000 salary increase.

It is a common experience that a problem difficult at night *is resolved in the morning* after the *committee of sleep* has worked on it.

John Steinbeck, *author*

> "Without enough sleep, we all become tall two-year-olds."
> JoJo Jensen, *Dirt Farmer Wisdom*

UNDERSTAND SLEEP BASICS

Sleep has five stages, some of which are repeated:

1. **Transition:** Ideally takes only 5 minutes or so for you to fall asleep.
2. **Light sleep:** Lasts 10 to 25 minutes. Your brain slows down, then ramps up, then slows down, as you transition into the next phase.
3. & 4. **Deep restorative (slow wave) sleep:** These two phases are the deepest stages; one transitions into the next. Blood flow is directed from your brain to your body. Brain waves dramatically slow; body regeneration ramps up. This stage repeats but decreases in duration as you sleep.
5. **REM sleep:** First occurs 70 to 90 minutes after you fall asleep. Arms and legs are still, and all focus is on brain restoration. This is also when you dream. REM sessions repeat and lengthen as you sleep. During REM sleep your brain:
   → Consolidates and processes everything you experienced that day.
   → Forms neural connections that strengthen and consolidate memory.
   → Replenishes the neurotransmitters, including dopamine and serotonin, which help all parts of your brain stay on track.
   → Fosters the ability of your brain to form new neurons and grow, known as plasticity.

If you don't get enough sleep, or your sleep is constantly interrupted, your brain may not have sufficient REM sleep, and therefore may not function at peak capacity.

MENTAL DEFICITS OF SLEEP DEPRIVATION

If you don't get sufficient sleep, your brain is not getting the restoration it needs. If you regularly don't get enough sleep, you may experience:

→ Fatigue, lethargy, and lack of motivation.
→ Reduced creativity and problem-solving skills.
→ Concentration and memory problems.
→ Difficulty making decisions.
→ Moodiness and irritability.

A sleep-deprived you obviously won't be operating at peak capacity, while a well-rested you will be more creative, energetic, focused, cooperative, cheerful, and productive.

5-MINUTE SABOTAGE LIST

If you are not getting 7 ½ to 9 hours of sleep a night, it's easy to find excellent advice online, at websites like Webmd.com. Meanwhile, it's very helpful to stop doing anything that requires focus (such as working) and turning off all electronic devices (TV, tablet, phone) at least one hour before bed. You don't want to worry about problems either, so it helps to create relaxation rituals, such as a warm shower or bath, reading (not in bed!), or meditating. Anything that helps you relax before you crawl beneath the sheets is a good idea.

TIP Meditation slows down your heart rate and lowers the levels of cortisol (the stress hormone) in your body, two things that happen naturally when you sleep. Meditation can also cause you to have theta brainwaves, the same state your brain enters when you are falling asleep.

Take five minutes and list five ways you know you sabotage your sleep.

1. _____
2. _____
3. _____
4. _____
5. _____

Now list five ideas for improving the quality of your sleep.

1. _____
2. _____
3. _____
4. _____
5. _____

 5-Minute Sleep Meditation

If your body tends to feel tense, a body-scan meditation can be helpful before sleep. Lie on your bed, close your eyes, breathe slowly in and out, focusing first on your breath, noticing only how it feels coming in and then leaving your body. After a minute, slowly move your attention to your entire body, and mentally scan your body from the tip of your head to your toes. Notice any areas of tension or pain, and mentally ask for relief; see if you can use your breath to expel the tension or pain. If a thought comes up connected to the pain, release it into the atmosphere. Keep doing this—slowly—until you feel relaxed and ready to sleep.

It's not just a question of

doing what you love for a living.

It is a matter of

doing what you love with love

Then your life *and all lives* will be transformed.

Rasheed Ogunlaru, *business coach*

Nurture Your Body

We all know that exercising and eating healthy are essential for a long happy life. If you want to be your best self and perform at peak capacity, moving your body every day will help improve blood flow to your brain and keep your energy levels high. Walking is one of the best exercises you can do; plus, it's known to improve creativity and relaxation. If you simply walk 7,000 steps a day, or briskly for 20 to 30 minutes three times a week, you'll be doing your body a favor. There's evidence that weight training is also good for your brain, as is anything that gets your heart rate up for short bursts of time.

Eating a variety of the foods from the essential food groups (protein, whole grains, vegetables, and fruits), while limiting sugar, salt, and bad fats is also crucial. Many doctors recommend the Mediterranean Diet, which is low in animal fats, high in whole grains, and includes plenty of vegetables, fruit, and nuts. Avoid saturated fats and processed foods as much as possible.

Simple Nutritional Basics

The U.S. Department of Agriculture recommends:

- Eating a variety of foods to maximize protein, vitamins, minerals, and fiber.
- Choosing plenty of whole-grain products, vegetables, and fruit.
- Choosing foods low in fat, saturated fat, and cholesterol.
- Limiting sugars (they're bad for your brain, as well as your weight).
- Limiting salt and sodium (which are bad for your blood pressure).
- Limiting alcohol or recreational drugs (which are very bad for your brain).

LIMIT SUGAR

The average American consumes 2 to 3 pounds of sugar each week; that's up from 5 pounds *per year* in the late 1880s (when heart disease and cancer were virtually unknown). Also, sugar thwarts optimal brain functioning by:

→ Slowing down neural communication;

→ Increasing inflammatory stress;

→ Interfering with synaptic communication;

→ Making neurons misfire and send erroneous messages;

→ Making it harder to think clearly;

→ Damaging your neurons.

Indulging in a high-sugar treat can make your stress hormones surge for as long as *5 hours*. These are reasons enough to limit your sugar intake, particularly if you want to be productive.

ADD BRAIN SUPERFOODS TO YOUR DAILY DIET

Superfoods provide essential nutrients that help you maintain your weight, fight disease, live longer, and function at your peak capacity. Here's a list of optimal brain superfoods:

→ Wild salmon, and other fish low in mercury (loaded with omega-3s).
→ Spinach, kale, broccoli, collards (brain-healthy nutrients may help slow cognitive decline).
→ Blueberries, acai, cranberries, goji, and boysenberries (loaded with antioxidants).
→ Walnuts, almonds, hazelnuts, pecans (good fats, but eat limited portions).
→ Quinoa (has amino acids that promote tissue growth and repair).
→ Eggs (have protein and good fat for the brain), but do your cholesterol a favor and limit to seven a week.
→ Oats (whole grains provide energy and fiber).
→ Soy (decreases blood clots and clumping).
→ Dark chocolate (70 percent cacao or more) provides flavanols (which improve learning and memory).

Hopefully the knowledge you've gained from reading this handbook and working through the exercises will help you become more productive and focused on what you can do to maximize the use of your time. As life always brings new challenges, it's been constructed to be a resource that you can revisit. With your new self-knowledge, a gameplan for moving forward, ways to improve brain function, and practical solutions, you should be well on your way to productivity.

Notes

Resources

Atomic Habits: An Easy & Proven Way to Build Good Habits & Break Bad Ones, James Clear (Avery, 2018).

Brainstorm: Harnessing the Power of Productive Obsessions, Eric Maisel, Ph.D. and Ann Maisel (New World Library, 2010).

Compulsive Procrastination: Some Self-Reported Characteristics, Joseph R. Ferrari, researcher (SAGE Journals, 1991).

Coping with Anxiety: 10 Simples Way to Relieve Anxiety, Fear & Worry, Edmund Bourne, Ph.D. (New Harbinger, 2016).

"Foods Linked to Better Brainpower," Harvard Health Publishing (March 6, 2021).

Grit to Great: How Perseverance, Passion, and Pluck Take You from Ordinary to Extraordinary, Linda Kaplan Thaler and Robin Koval (Crown Business, 2015).

How to Own Your Own Mind, Napoleon Hill (TarcherPerigee, 2017).

Magnificent Mind at Any Age: Natural Ways to Unleash Your Brain's Maximum Potential, Daniel G. Amen, M.D. (Three Rivers Press, 2008).

Meditation for Moms: How to Relax Your Body, Refresh Your Mind, and Revitalize Your Spirit, Kim Dwyer and Susan Reynolds (Adams Media, 2012).

"Meditation Is Common across Many Religious Groups in the U.S.," David Masci and Conrad Hackett. Pew Research Center (January 2, 2018).

"The Nature of Procrastination: A Meta-Analytic and Theoretical Review of Quintessential Self-Regulatory Failure," Piers Steel. *Psychological Bulletin*, 133(1) (2007).

"Neuroscience Explains Why You Need to Write Down Your Goals if You Actually Want to Achieve Them," Mark Murphy. *Forbes* (April 15, 2018).

Peak Mind: Fine Your Focus, Own Your Attention, Invest 12 Minutes a Day, Amishi P. Jha, Ph.D. (Harper Collins, 2021).

Procrastination, Health & Well-Being, Timothy Pychyl, Ph.D., with Dr. Fuschia Sirois (Elsevier Academic Press, 2016).

"Procrastination's Impact in the Workplace and the Workplace's Impact on Procrastination," Brenda Nguyen and Piers Steel, *International Journal of Selection and Assessment*, 21(4) (2013).

Solving the Procrastination Puzzle: A Concise Guide to Strategies for Change, Timothy Pychyl, Ph.D. (TarcherPerigee/Penguin, 2013).

Stop Avoiding Stuff: 25 Microskills to Face Your Fears & Do It Anyway, Matthew S. Boone, LCSW, Jennifer Gregg Ph.D., and Lisa Coyne, Ph.D. (New Harbinger, 2020).

The Success Principles: How to Get from Where You Are to Where You Want to Be, Jack Canfield (William Morrow, 2015).

Train Your Brain to Get Rich, Teresa Aubele, Ph.D. and Susan Reynolds (Adams Media, 2011).

Train Your Mind Change Your Brain: How a New Science Reveals Our Extraordinary Potential to Transform Ourselves, Sharon Begley (Ballantine Books, 2007).

"Why Cognitive Behavioral Therapy Is the Current Gold Standard of Psychotherapy," Daniel David, Ioana Cristea, and Stefan G. Hofmann, *Frontiers in Psychiatry* (2018).

"25 Trending Remote Work Statistics [2022]: Facts, Trends, and Projections," Jack Flynn. Zippia (October 16, 2022).

"28 of the Very Best Planners," Dominique Pariso. *New York Magazine* (August 17, 2022).

Inspiring | Educating | Creating | Entertaining

Brimming with creative inspiration, how-to projects, and useful information to enrich your everyday life, quarto.com is a favorite destination for those pursuing their interests and passions.

© 2023 Quarto Publishing Group USA Inc.

This edition published in 2023 by Chartwell Books,
an imprint of The Quarto Group
142 West 36th Street, 4th Floor
New York, NY 10018 USA
T (212) 779-4972 F (212) 779-6058
www.Quarto.com

10 9 8 7 6 5 4 3 2 1

Chartwell titles are also available at discount for retail, wholesale, promotional, and bulk purchase. For details, contact the Special Sales Manager by email at specialsales@quarto.com or by mail at The Quarto Group, Attn: Special Sales Manager, 100 Cummings Center Suite 265D, Beverly, MA 01915, USA.

ISBN: 978-0-7858-4205-7

Publisher: Wendy Friedman
Senior Managing Editor: Meredith Mennitt
Senior Design Manager: Michael Caputo
Editor: Jennifer Kushnier
Designer: Kate Sinclair

All stock design elements ©Shutterstock

Printed in China

This book provides general information. It should not be relied upon as recommending or promoting any specific diagnosis or method of treatment for a particular condition. It is not intended as a substitute for medical advice or for direct diagnosis and treatment of a medical or psychological condition by a qualified physician or therapist. Readers who have questions about a particular condition, possible treatments for that condition, or possible reactions from the condition or its treatment should consult a physician, therapist, or other qualified healthcare professional.